A+
PC Technician's
Pocket Reference

James F. Kelly and Brian Schwarz

McGraw-Hill/Osborne

New York   Chicago   San Francisco
Lisbon   London   Madrid   Mexico City   Milan
New Delhi   San Juan   Seoul   Singapore   Sydney   Toronto

The *McGraw·Hill* Companies

McGraw-Hill/Osborne
2100 Powell Street, Floor 10
Emeryville, California 94608
U.S.A.

To arrange bulk purchase discounts for sales promotions,
premiums, or fund-raisers, please contact **McGraw-Hill**/Osborne
at the above address. For information on translations or book
distributors outside the U.S.A., please see the International
Contact Information page immediately following the index of
this book.

A+ PC Technician's Pocket Reference

Publisher   Brandon A. Nordin
Vice President & Associate Publisher   Scott Rogers
Acquisitions Editor   Franny Kelly
Project Editor   Lisa Wolters-Broder
Acquisitions Coordinator   Jessica Wilson
Technical Editor   Doris Pavlichek
Copy Editor   Bill McManus
Proofreaders   Susie Elkind, Lisa Wolters-Broder
Indexer   Claire Splan
Computer Designers   Lucie Ericksen, Elizabeth Jang
Illustrators   Michael Mueller, Lyssa Wald, Melinda Moore Lytle
Series Design   Peter F. Hancik
Cover Series Design   Jeff Weeks

1234567890 DOC DOC 019876543

ISBN 0-07-222905-5

This book was composed with Corel VENTURA™ Publisher.

To Mom and Dad, who never raised an eyebrow
when I paused my engineering studies
to get that English degree.

—Jim

About the Authors

James F. Kelly is currently co-owner of Those Computer People, Inc., a Houston, Texas-based company that provides its clients with a variety of technology services. He received a B.S. in industrial engineering from Florida State University and a B.A. in English from the University of West Florida. Technical jobs led to technical editing, which led him to technical writing.

Brian Schwarz is a technical trainer and co-author of *Network+ Certification All-in-One Exam Guide* from McGraw-Hill/Osborne.

About the Technical Reviewer

Doris E. Pavlichek is the author of *Cisco Internetwork Design* (McGraw-Hill/Osborne, 2001) and co-author of *Juniper Networks Reference Guide: JUNOS Routing, Configuration and Architecture* (Addison-Wesley, 2002). Formerly a technical project manager and network engineer, she currently uses her skills as a freelance writer and editor, producing marketing material and web content for businesses. Doris resides in Maryland with her husband, children, and menagerie of pets.

CONTENTS @ A GLANCE

CONTENTS

ACKNOWLEDGMENTS

A *huge* thanks go out to Lisa Wolters-Broder, Jessica Wilson, and Doris Pavlichek for all their help in keeping me focused on the project.

A *special* thank you to Franny Kelly. He had faith that I could do this, and I am in his debt for giving me a shot.

Extra special thanks to Mike Meyers—also known as A+ Guru of the Universe—for lending us artwork from his previous works.

And finally, thanks to Brian Schwarz, my co-author. It was fun!

INTRODUCTION

In keeping with the idea of a pocket reference book, this introduction will be "pocket-sized."

The book you're holding in your hands serves many purposes. One that comes to mind is that it provides a nice summary and quick study for those wishing to pursue the A+ exam that CompTIA administers. Another is that it provides a quick review of basic technologies and terminology for those of us who have (possibly) forgotten more than we're willing to admit. It happens.

The book is by no means comprehensive. There is simply no possible way to include every technology related to PC hardware and software and keep the book from approaching encyclopedia-sized volumes.

It's a pocket reference; therefore the authors have attempted to cover those topics that they feel are important to the A+ exam. But coverage is also given to day-to-day troubleshooting that A+ technicians and others encounter regularly.

Chapters are short for a reason; we've attempted to whittle down the topics to their core. The chapters will give you useful information, but a lot of that information is there to jog your memory.

Most technicians know where to find advanced information, but sometimes all you need are the basics. Most technicians will admit that many times "the" solution is the simplest one. This book gives you those simple solutions.

If you're planning on taking the A+ exam—good luck! Review the sticky subjects before you head into the testing center, and give this book a quick thumb-through before handing over your study materials.

And if you've passed the A+ exam, don't count on remembering every little bit of information that you've crammed. With the IT industry changing daily (almost hourly), there's simply no way to remember everything. Keep a copy of this book on your desk or in your back pocket. Those of us in this industry know that sooner or later, the simple stuff comes back around to test us.

Part I

Ports and Connectors

Chapter 1

Peripheral Ports and Connectors

Serial Ports

Serial ports transfer data 1 bit at a time. Typical uses include:

- Mice
- External modems
- Connecting to networking hardware such as routers

Serial ports come in two forms, a 9-pin male connector and a 25-pin male connector. Most new PCs ship with the 9-pin variation, shown in Figure 1-1, but adapters are available.

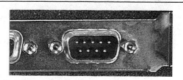

Figure 1-1. A 9-pin serial port

Parallel Ports

Parallel ports transfer data 8 bits at a time. Typical uses include:

- Printers
- Mass storage devices such as Zip drives and external CD-ROM drives
- Low-end scanners

Parallel ports use a 25-pin female connection, like the one shown in Figure 1-2.

CAUTION *A 25-pin female connection can also be a SCSI connector.*

Universal Serial Bus (USB) Connectors

USB connectors provide a serial interface for connecting a wide variety of peripherals, including:

- Mice
- Scanners
- Keyboards
- Cameras
- Microphones

Figure 1-2. A 25-pin parallel port

- Joysticks and game controllers

- Network interfaces

Advantages of USB over standard serial and parallel
connections include:

- **Hot-swappable**   Devices can be connected or
  disconnected without shutting down the PC.

- **Speed**   USB 1.0 devices can operate at speeds up to
  12 Mbps, while the newer USB 2.0 devices operate at
  speeds up to 480 Mbps.

- **Expandability**   Up to 127 USB devices can be
  connected in a single chain (although the practical
  limit depends on the specific devices used).

- **Power**   The USB cable can provide power to devices
  that require less than 500 mA (milliamps), eliminating
  the need for many cables.

USB devices can attach directly to the PC, to other USB
devices, or to USB hubs, such as the ones shown in
Figures 1-3 and 1-4.

Figure 1-3.   A USB hub

Figure 1-4. USB male and female connectors

Keyboard, Mouse, and PS/2 Connectors—the DIN Connectors

Although keyboards and mice can use USB connectors, most PCs still use DIN connectors. Older PCs use the larger 5-pin DIN connector (Figure 1-5) for the keyboard, while newer PCs typically use the smaller 6-pin mini-DIN connector (Figure 1-6) for both keyboards and mice. The

Figure 1-5. AT-style DIN connector (5-pin)

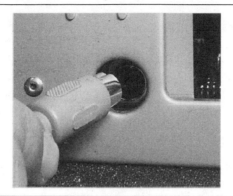

Figure 1-6. 6-pin mini-DIN (PS/2) connector

6-pin mini-DIN connector is more commonly known as a PS/2 connector, and the 5-pin connector is sometimes referred to as an AT-style connector.

Video

VGA, SVGA, and XVGA monitors connect to the PC using a 15-pin, three-row DB connector. The cable has a male connector, and the corresponding connector on the PC is female, as shown in Figure 1-7.

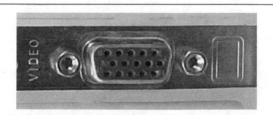

Figure 1-7. A female VGA video connection

Sound

PC sound cards use miniature audio jacks to connect speakers, microphones, and other audio devices. A typical soundcard has two or more jacks, identical in appearance, labeled by function: microphone, speaker, line out, or line in.

Game Ports/MIDI Ports

Game and MIDI (Musical Instrument Digital Interface) ports use a 15-pin, two-row connector. On most sound cards, the same physical port can perform either function, acting as either a game or MIDI port, as shown in Figure 1-8.

CAUTION *On older PCs, you will sometimes find an identical 15-pin, two-row connector used for an older and rarely seen Ethernet connector. If the connector appears as part of a sound card, it is a game/MIDI port. If it appears on a network card, perhaps adjacent to an RJ-45 or BNC connector, it is an Ethernet connector.*

Figure 1-8.   Sound cards with miniature audio jacks and game ports

Modems

Modems use the same RJ-11 connector (Figure 1-9) used on standard U.S. telephone jacks.

Network Interface Cards (NICs)

The network connections on the back of the PC correspond to the cabling used. Common network connections, also shown in Figure 1-10, include:

- **RJ-45** Eight-wire connector commonly used with unshielded twisted pair (UTP) cable for both Ethernet and Token Ring networks.

- **BNC** Used with RG-58 coaxial cable for 10Base2 Ethernet networks (also known as thin Ethernet).

- **AUI** A 15-pin, two-row DB connector used with RG-8 coaxial cable and an external transceiver for 10Base5 Ethernet networks (also known as thick Ethernet).

- **Type 1** Used for Token Ring networks using shielded twisted pair (STP) cable; see Figure 1-11.

Figure 1-9.   RJ-11 connections on a modem

Figure 1-10. Ethernet cards with the common network connections: BNC and RJ-45 (top), AUI and RJ-45 (middle), and BNC, AUI, and RJ-45 (bottom)

Ethernet cards often have more than one type of physical connection.

CAUTION *When using BNC connectors, attach the cable to the NIC using a T-connector (Figure 1-12). Connecting the cable directly to the BNC connector on the NIC will not work.*

Figure 1-11. Type 1 connector

Figure 1-12.   Use a T-connector with 10Base2

Printers

Printers can use a variety of connectors, including:

- **Centronics** A 36-pin connector (see Figure 1-13). The typical cable has a Centronics connector on one end that plugs into the printer and a male DB25 connector on the other end that connects to a parallel port on the PC.

- **USB** Many printers offer both a USB connector and a Centronics connector for backward compatibility with older systems. USB printers typically require an additional power supply.

- **Ethernet** High-end printers often offer a built-in network connection using an RJ-45 connector.

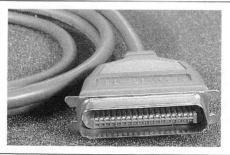

Figure 1-13.   36-pin Centronics connector

FireWire/IEEE 1394

IEEE 1394, also known as FireWire (see Figure 1-14), provides a high-speed connection for bandwidth-hungry devices such as external drives and video devices. FireWire devices can operate at speeds up to 400 Mbps.

Figure 1-14.   FireWire (IEEE 1394) connector

Chapter 2

Cleaning Your PC

Cleaning Solutions

Avoid damage to the PC by always using the correct supplies when cleaning the PC. Household cleaners such as glass cleaner can harm some PC components, including laptop screens. Table 2-1 lists which cleaning supplies to use when cleaning various parts of a PC.

CAUTION *Always turn off the PC before using liquid cleaners.*

Water	Apply with damp (but not wet) cloth to clean the outside of the computer case and monitor. Add a mild soap to the water if necessary.
Denatured alcohol	Use denatured alcohol to clean dirty contacts. It will evaporate and leave no residue.
Glass cleaner	While glass cleaner can be used to clean CRT screens, never use it on LCD screens because it can melt the screen.
Fabric softener	Use a mix of one part fabric softener to ten parts water on the exterior of the PC as a cleaning solution and antistatic measure.

Table 2-1.   Cleaning Solutions

CAUTION *Do not use pencil erasers to clean contacts—erasers can leave a residue and damage the contacts.*

Cleaning Tools

Household appliances such as standard vacuum cleaners create static discharges that can damage the PC. Table 2-2 lists which types of tools you can use to clean a PC.

CAUTION *Do not use the "dry dusting" cloths on your PC, such as Swiffer Sweeper, because they use static electricity to pick up dust.*

CAUTION *Never use a standard household vacuum cleaner on your PC.*

Nonstatic vacuum cleaner	Remove dust from the case and keyboard with a specially made vacuum cleaner that does not produce static.
Compressed air	Use a can of compressed air to blow dust out of hard-to-reach areas, such as the PC power supply fan. Use caution and always hold the can upright. Otherwise, the liquid propellant in the can could destroy some components.
Lint-free cloths	Lint-free cloths, such as those used for cleaning eyeglasses, can be used for removing dust from the PC.

Table 2-2. Cleaning Tools

Chapter 3

Technician's Toolkit

The Technician's Toolkit

Most computer and office supply stores carry basic PC toolkits, but the contents vary. Use this list as a guide for assembling your personal toolkit.

A minimal kit should include:

- Phillips head screwdriver
- Standard screwdriver
- Tweezers
- Boot disk or CD for each supported operating system
- Spare parts tube with screws and spare jumper shunts
- Voltmeter
- Antistatic wrist strap

A full tool kit should also include:

- Needle-nose pliers
- 3/16-inch nut driver
- Torx (star-shaped) screwdrivers
- Small flashlight
- Wire cutters
- Can of compressed air
- Lint-free cleaning cloth
- Denatured alcohol
- Installation CDs for each supported operating system

- Driver CDs for supported hardware
- RJ-45 crimping tool and spare connectors
- PDI card (POST, DMA, and IRQ diagnostic card)
- Flashlight

Spare Parts

Ideally, a technician should have spares for every component of a PC on hand to minimize downtime. At a minimum, keep spares for commonly used and relatively inexpensive parts:

- Ribbon cables for floppy, IDE, and SCSI devices
- Floppy drive
- Network card
- PCI 56 Kbps modem
- Cat 5 patch cable
- Cat 5 crossover cable
- RJ-11 telephone cable
- Keyboard
- Mouse
- Power supply
- Molex power splitter

If possible, keep spares of additional components, including hard drives, CD drives, motherboards, RAM, and CPUs.

Chapter 4

Power

Outlet Voltages

Standard U.S. electrical power outlets (see Figure 4-1)
provide 115V, 60 Hz AC power. You can test the connection
using a standard voltmeter. When wired correctly, the
outlet should return the approximate values listed in
Table 4-2 when tested with a voltmeter.

PC Power Supply

The PC power supply converts AC power into DC power of
various voltages required by devices in the PC, including
the CPU, motherboard, hard drives, etc.

Power supplies come in two major varieties: AT and ATX.

AT Power Supplies

AT power supplies connect to the motherboard with two
6-wire connectors, called P8 and P9. When connecting P8
and P9 to the motherboard, be certain to keep the black
ground wires together, as shown in Figure 4-2.

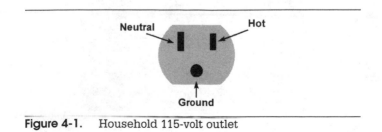

Figure 4-1. Household 115-volt outlet

electricity	A flow of negatively charged particles, called electrons, through matter.
conductors	Materials in which electrons move freely.
current	Amount of electrons moving past a point on the wire; measured in amperes.
ampere (A or amp)	A unit of measure of the rate of electron flow or current in an electrical conductor.
voltage	Electrical pressure, the force that causes current to flow through a conductor.
volt (V)	A unit of measure for voltage.
alternating current (AC)	Electrons flow back and forth, alternating at a frequency that is measured in hertz.
direct current (DC)	Electrons flow in one direction around a continuous circuit.
power supply	In a PC, a device that converts AC power to low-voltage DC power.
hertz (Hz)	Cycles per second.
watt (W)	Unit of measure for power.
joule (J)	Unit of measure for work.

Table 4-1. Electrical Definitions

Figure 4-2. Properly connected P8 and P9 connectors

Positive Lead	Negative Lead	Result
Hot	Neutral	~115V
Hot	Ground	~115V
Neutral	Ground	0V

Table 4-2. Proper Values Returned by a Voltmeter when Testing a Standard U.S. AC Outlet

Table 4-3 shows the voltages for each wire in the P8 and P9 connectors.

4

CAUTION *Connecting the P8 and P9 connectors backwards can damage the PC.*

ATX Power Supplies

ATX power supplies use a single P1 connector to supply power to the motherboard. This 20-wire, two-row connector uses a notched connector and can only be connected one way, as shown in Figure 4-3.

Pin	Color	Function
p8-1	Orange	Power good
p8-2	Red	+5V
p8-3	Yellow	+12V
p8-4	Blue	−12V
p8-5	Black	Ground
p8-6	Black	Ground
p9-1	Black	Ground
p9-2	Black	Ground
p9-3	White	−5V
p9-4	Red	+5V
p9-5	Red	+5V
p9-6	Red	+5V

Table 4-3. Pin-out for P8 and P9 Connectors

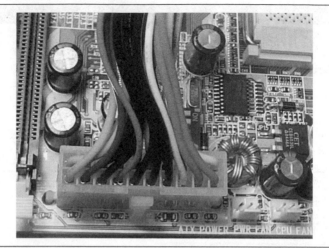

Figure 4-3. A properly connected P1 connector

Table 4-4 shows the voltage for each wire in the two-row P1 connector.

Pin	Color	Function	Pin	Color	Function
11	Orange Brown	+3.3V +3.3V sense	1	Orange	+3.3V
12	Blue	−12V	2	Orange	+3.3V
13	Black	Ground	3	Black	Ground
14	Green	ps_on	4	Red	+5V
15	Black	Ground	5	Black	Ground
16	Black	Ground	6	Red	+5V
17	Black	Ground	7	Black	Ground
18	White	−5V	8	Gray	pwr_ok
19	Red	+5V	9	Purple	+5V
20	Red	+5V	10	Yellow	+12V

Table 4-4. ATX Power Supply P1 Connector Pin-out

CAUTION When using an ATX motherboard with the soft-power option, the power supply provides a trickle of electricity to the motherboard even when the PC is "off." To work inside the PC, be sure to unplug the power supply and wait several seconds to ensure that the PC is fully powered down.

Molex and Mini Connectors

Both AT and ATX power supplies use the same standard Molex (Figure 4-4) and mini connectors (Figure 4-6) for supplying power to peripherals. Molex and mini connectors can supply both +5V and +12V. Figure 4-5 shows the voltages for the Molex connector, and Figure 4-6 shows the voltages for the mini connector.

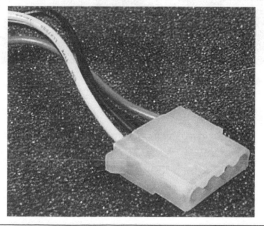

Figure 4-4. Molex connector

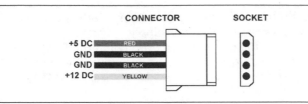

Figure 4-5. Molex connector and socket diagram

Figure 4-6. Mini connector

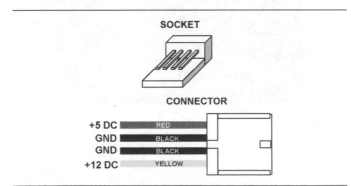

Figure 4-7. Mini connector and socket diagram

Surge Suppressors

The PC power supply itself provides some surge suppression, but uses an external surge suppressor for additional protection. When using a modem, use a surge suppressor that protects the PC from phone line power surges as well.

When purchasing a surge suppressor, be sure that it meets the following minimum standards:

- UL 1449 for 330V rating

- 800 joules (or more)

- UL 497A rating for modem surge suppression (if applicable)

CAUTION   *Typical surge suppressors protect against minor fluctuations in power, not against major surges such as those caused by electrical storms. For safety, unplug the PC and modem from the wall to protect your PC during electrical storms.*

Uninterruptible Power Supply

An uninterruptible power supply (UPS) provides a battery backup for the PC, and provides some protection from both power surges and power sags. In the event of a blackout, a UPS allows a technician to shut down the PC gracefully.

The typical UPS acts as a standby power system (SPS), using the battery to power the PC only when the unit detects a power sag. An online UPS provides a more comprehensive solution, running the PC off of the UPS battery at all times to ensure consistent power. An online UPS, however, costs significantly more.

Fire Extinguishers and Electricity

Only use class C fire extinguishers on electrical fires. Table 4-5 lists the types of fires for which each of the three classes of fire extinguishers should be used.

Class	Use on:
Class A	Ordinary combustible solids, such as wood or paper
Class B	Flammable liquids, such as gasoline, solvents, or oil-based paints
Class C	Electrical fires

Table 4-5. Classes of Fire Extinguishers

Chapter 5

Disposal

In general, computer components cannot be disposed of with regular waste because of the toxic chemicals they contain. The disposal of batteries, CRTs, and circuit boards in particular require special attention.

Batteries

Laptop computers use three main types of batteries:

- Nickel-Cadmium (NiCad) batteries have fallen into disfavor for laptop batteries because they contain high levels of toxic chemicals. Many older devices reaching the end of their useful lives use these batteries.

- Nickel Metal Hydride (NiMH) batteries provide a less toxic alternative to NiCad batteries. While less toxic than the earlier NiCad batteries, these should still be disposed of separately.

- Lithium Ion (LiIon) batteries have become the preferred choice for many devices because LiIon batteries provide significantly longer battery life.

None of these battery types should be disposed of with regular trash. Contact your local waste management authority to locate a recycling center that will accept your old batteries, or consult the Rechargeable Battery Recycling Corporation (RBRC) online at www.rbrc.org/ to find a battery recycling center near you.

***

CAUTION *Never incinerate batteries. In addition to releasing toxic chemicals, batteries can explode when subjected to extreme heat.*

CRT

The CRT monitors used by most desktop computers contain several pounds of lead, a toxic substance. CRTs should never be disposed of in the regular trash. Consult your local waste management authority for more information.

Circuit Boards and Other Components

The circuit boards and other components inside PCs and other electronic components contain significant amounts of toxic chemicals, including lead, mercury, and cadmium. Do not dispose of computer components with the regular trash. Consult your local waste management authority for more information about proper disposal of these items.

CAUTION   *When working with other chemicals, compounds, or components, consult the items' Material Safety Data Sheets (MSDSs) for warnings, safe disposal requirements, and safe methods of transportation. Contact the manufacturer if a MSDS did not come with an item.*

Chapter 6

Electrostatic Discharge (ESD)

Electrostatic Discharge (ESD)

Electrostatic discharge, commonly known as ESD, refers
to the discharge of static electricity that occurs when
two objects with different electrical potentials come into
contact. ESD can damage a PC in two ways:

6

- **Catastrophic ESD** The computer fails immediately.

- **Hidden ESD** Static build-up on the PC causes a PC
  component to behave erratically.

Be aware that ESD damage can be cumulative—many small
shocks can add up to significant damage.

ESD Protection Devices
for Working on the PC

When properly used, the following devices can help
protect the PC from ESD damage:

- Antistatic wrist and ankle straps

- Antistatic mats

- Antistatic floor mats

- Antistatic bags

- Antistatic sprays (not recommended—can damage
  PC components)

In addition to these devices, many technicians make a
habit of touching the exterior of the PC power supply
before working inside the PC to safely discharge static
electricity.

Preventing ESD

Friction, such as the friction between shoes and carpet, can cause a buildup of electrical potential in the human body, especially in conditions of low humidity. You can reduce the likelihood of ESD damage to PC components by doing the following:

- Wearing natural fibers (cotton, linen, wool) while working on the PC

- Wearing rubber-soled shoes

- Using a work area with linoleum or uncarpeted floors

- Keeping long hair tied back

- Removing rings and other jewelry

CAUTION *The steps listed above protect the equipment, not the technician. Do not ground yourself when working on high-voltage equipment such as the inside of CRT monitors or the inside of a power supply.*

Electromagnetic Interference (EMI)

Electromagnetic interference describes interference generated by the magnetic fields of other devices. EMI can originate from devices inside the PC or from external sources such as refrigerators and televisions. Unlike ESD, EMI will not normally cause damage to your PC, but it can interfere with its normal operation. Devices such as stereo speakers and refrigerators that generate high levels of EMI should be kept at a distance from your PC.

TIP *Don't confuse EMI (electromagnetic interference) with ESD (electrostatic discharge).*

Chapter 7

Motherboards

Motherboard Form Factors

PC motherboards come in two form factors, AT and ATX. Newer computers use the ATX form factor to take advantage of its additional connectors, but many AT motherboards remain in use. Table 7-1 summarizes the key differences between AT and ATX motherboards.

AT and "Baby AT"

The AT form factor defines standard locations for screw holes and a 5-pin AT-style DIN keyboard connector. The original AT motherboard measured 12×13 inches, but most AT motherboards in use today use the "baby AT" form factor of 8.5×13 inches. Figure 7-1 shows a typical AT motherboard.

Form Factor	Power Connector	Connections	Size (inches)
AT	P8 and P9	Keyboard (5 pin AT-style DIN)	12×13 or 8.5×13
ATX	P1	Floppy drive Primary and secondary IDE controllers Keyboard (PS/2 style) Mouse (PS/2 style) Parallel (25 pin) Serial (9 pin) USB Sound	12×9.6

Table 7-1. AT and ATX Motherboard Summary

Figure 7-1. An AT motherboard

ATX

ATX motherboards offer an improved layout and standard locations for many common integrated connections (see Figure 7-2). The ATX standard does not specify which connections should be integrated on the motherboard. Instead, the standard specifies their placement if the manufacturer chooses to include them. Figure 7-3 shows typical connections on an ATX motherboard.

The design of an ATX motherboard provides better access to components and better airflow than an AT motherboard.

ATX motherboards also feature "soft power," meaning the motherboard remains powered on even when the system is "off." Soft power provides support for enhanced power management features. Aside from supporting features such as suspend, resume, and hibernate, soft power enables the operating system to turn the system off when shutting down.

Figure 7-2. An ATX motherboard

CAUTION *Because ATX motherboards support soft power, parts of the system remain powered on whenever the system is plugged in. Always unplug an ATX system before performing any work inside the case.*

Figure 7-3. ATX ports

Selecting a Motherboard

When selecting a motherboard, be certain to consult the accompanying documentation, also known as the *motherboard book.* The motherboard book will list all supported CPUs. In addition to requiring the appropriate socket or slot, CPUs require specific voltages and other support features from the motherboard. The motherboard book will also specify the types and amount of RAM supported.

CAUTION *Do not assume that a CPU will work with a particular motherboard simply because it fits—check the motherboard book first!*

Integrated Peripherals

Modern motherboards typically include integrated floppy and IDE disk controllers, but many motherboards incorporate other peripherals such as sound, video, USB, and even FireWire.

CAUTION *You may wish to add a high-performance sound or video card to a system that already has these features integrated into the motherboard. If so, be certain to disable the integrated peripherals in the system BIOS before installing the new device. If you forget to disable the integrated peripheral, the new device may simply not be recognized by the system or the entire system may lock up.*

The Wires

Both AT and ATX motherboards have connections for several wires that should be attached to the front panel of the computer case (see Figure 7-4). These wires include:

- Soft power (ATX only)
- Power LED
- Reset
- Speaker
- Hard drive activity light
- Keylock (less common in ATX)
- Turbo and Turbo LED (AT only, generally nonfunctional even when present)

While only the soft power wire needs to be connected for the PC to boot up (you cannot turn on an ATX motherboard without it), you should properly connect all of them. Sometimes the reset switch is very handy!

TIP *The LEDs have a positive and negative side—they won't work if you plug them in backward. Fortunately, plugging these wires in backward will not damage anything.*

7

Figure 7-4.   Sample front panel wires

Chapter 8

Expansion Buses

ISA

The ISA (Industry Standard Architecture) bus, available
in 8- and 16-bit versions, provides an adequate interface
for devices that do not require high performance. While
acceptable for devices such as modems, the lack of native
Plug and Play (PnP) support makes ISA a poor choice
for newer systems. While many working systems have
ISA slots, they have virtually disappeared from new
motherboards. Figure 8-1 shows a typical 16-bit ISA slot.

CAUTION *In systems using ISA devices, be prepared
to troubleshoot IRQ, I/O address, and DMA channel
problems. Even ISA devices that claim to support Plug
and Play can cause problems.*

PCI

Available in both 32- and 64-bit versions, the PCI
(Peripheral Component Interconnect) bus provides a

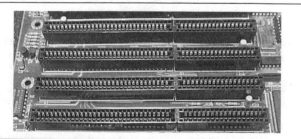

Figure 8-1.   16-bit ISA slot

high-performance bus capable of supporting most current devices. PCI devices fully support Plug and Play. PCI also supports the following:

- **Bus mastering**   PCI devices can transfer data between themselves if the CPU is not communicating with another PCI device.

- **Burst mode**   PCI devices can transfer data efficiently, eliminating extraneous address information and sending data in bursts rather than addressing each byte individually.

Most desktop PCs use the 32-bit version of PCI. Manufacturers typically reserve the 64-bit version for use in their server-class systems. Figure 8-2 shows a typical 32-bit PCI slot.

AGP

AGP (Accelerated Graphics Port) provides a dedicated data bus for video. By separating video from the PCI bus, AGP provides improved video performance and frees up additional bandwidth for devices using the PCI bus. AGP supports system memory access, a technique that enables an AGP card to use portions of the system memory for certain tasks. Figure 8-3 shows a typical AGP slot.

Figure 8-2.   PCI slot

Figure 8-3.   An AGP slot

CAUTION   Don't confuse system memory access with unified memory architecture (UMA), a technology that uses system memory for all video tasks. Used as a cost-savings measure, UMA-based video cards (usually integrated into the motherboard) deliver significantly lower video performance. High-performance video cards require much higher-performance RAM than the RAM normally used for the main system memory. For light office tasks, a PC using UMA may be acceptable, but be aware of the trade-off between price and performance.

Comparison of Expansion Buses

Table 8-1 summarizes the key features of the common expansion buses.

Bus	Data Path Width	Data Transfer Rate	PnP	Notes
ISA	8/16	5.33/8.33 MB/s	No	Original PC expansion bus
PCI (32 bit)	32	132 MB/s	Yes	Common expansion bus used in modern PCs
PCI (64 bit)	64	264 MB/s	Yes	Typically found in server-class machines for high-performance components
AGP 2x	32	533 MB/s	Yes	Provides dedicated data path for video
AGP 4x	64	1 GB/s	Yes	Provides dedicated data path for video
AGP 8x	64	2.1 GB/s	Yes	Provides dedicated data path for video

Table 8-1. Common Expansion Buses

Obsolete Expansion Bus Technologies

While not found in new machines, manufacturers who needed a high-performance expansion bus before the introduction of the PCI bus used either a Microchannel (MCA) or VESA local bus (VLB) expansion bus. Some of these older systems (see Table 8-2) remain in use, although they are becoming increasingly rare.

Bus	Data Path Width	Data Transfer Rate (MB/s)	PnP	Notes
MCA	16/32/64	20/40/80/160	No; used proprietary self-configuration mechanism	Obsolete; mostly used in older IBM-branded PCs
VLB	32/64	132/264	No	Obsolete; mostly confined to 486 class computers, but occasionally appears in early Pentium-based systems

Table 8-2. Obsolete Expansion Buses

Next-Generation Expansion Bus Technologies

PCI and AGP have been the "gold standard" for PC expansion busses for several years, but prepare for the next generation of expansion buses, including PCI-X 2.0, PCI Express, InfiniBand, and HyperTransport.

The eventual winner among these competing technologies remains unclear. In the future, we may see standard desktop PCs incorporating all or none of these technologies. Consult Table 8-3 for links to additional information about these new technologies.

Bus	Data Transfer Rate (GB/s)	For More Information
PCI-X 2.0	1	www.pcisig.com/specifications/pcix_20
PCI Express	16	www.pcisig.com/specifications/pciexpress
InfiniBand	2.5	www.infinibandta.org/ibta/
HyperTransport	12.8	www.hypertransport.org/

Table 8-3. Next-Generation Expansion Buses

Chapter 9

BIOS

BIOS (Basic Input/Output System) consists of a set of programs that enable communication with the basic hardware of the PC. Modern PCs use a reprogrammable flash ROM chip to store the BIOS, enabling PC technicians to upgrade the BIOS without physically replacing the chip. The BIOS also provides the program known as the power-on self test (POST).

POST

During the boot process, the POST checks the basic hardware components of the PC. In the event of an error, the user is alerted by either a beep code or a text message.

Beep Codes

PCs use beep codes to report errors that occur before the video initializes. The beep codes vary depending on the manufacturer of the BIOS and change over time (see Tables 9-1, 9-2, and 9-3 for examples). Consult your BIOS manufacturer's web site for the most current information.

TIP *Beep codes can sometimes result from power problems. If the beep codes are intermittent, investigate power problems before worrying about the low-level errors indicated by the specific beep codes.*

TIP *When in doubt, reseating all components (RAM, CPU, PCI, ISA cards, and so on) will resolve many beep code errors.*

Beeps	POST Routine Description
1	Refresh failure
2	Parity error
3	Base K memory failure
4	Timer not operational
5	Processor error
6	8042 – gate A20 error
7	Processor exception interrupt error
8	Display memory read/write error
9	ROM checksum error
10	CMOS shutdown register read/write error
11	Cache memory bad

Table 9-1. AMI BIOS 4.5 Beep Codes

Beeps	POST Routine Description
1-2-2-3	BIOS ROM checksum
1-3-1-1	Test DRAM refresh
1-3-1-3	Test 8742 keyboard controller
1-3-4-1	RAM failure on address line xxxx
1-2-4-3	RAM failure on data bits xxxx of low byte of memory bus
2-1-2-3	Test for unexpected interrupts
2-2-3-1	Test for unexpected interrupts
1-2	Search for option ROMs; one long, two short beeps on checksum failure
1	One short beep before boot (indicating normal bootup process is starting)

Table 9-2. Phoenix BIOS 4.0 Release 6.x Beep Codes

Problem	Possible Solution
RAM refresh failure Parity error RAM bit error	Reseat and clean the RAM chips. Replace individual chips until problem is corrected.
Base 64 K error	Replace chips with non-parity if supported.
8042 or error Gate A20 error	Reseat and clean keyboard chip. Replace keyboard. Replace motherboard.
BIOS checksum error	Reseat and clean ROM chip.
Video error	Reseat video card. Replace video card.
Cache memory error	Reseat and clean cache chips. Verify cache jumper or CMOS settings. Replace cache chips.
Everything else	Clean motherboard. Replace motherboard.

Table 9-3. Common POST Beep Errors and Solutions

Numeric Error Codes

Although generally replaced by more self-explanatory
text messages, numeric error codes still appear on some
systems. Table 9-4 outlines these error codes.

Error Code	Problem
201	Memory error
301	Keyboard error
1701	Hard drive controller error
7301	Floppy drive controller error
161	Dead battery
1101	Serial card error

Table 9-4. Numeric Error Codes

CAUTION   Remember that inconsistent errors on boot generally indicate power problems, not the problem indicated by the error code. Reboot the system several times to determine if the same error repeats before taking drastic measures such as replacing hardware.

Chapter 10

CMOS

PCs store configuration CMOS settings; this is information about the basic PC hardware, including:

- CPU speed and multiplier
- IDE drives
- Floppy drives
- Settings for onboard connectors such as parallel and serial ports.

NOTE *Although most current motherboards store these settings on a flash ROM, most technicians typically refer to them as CMOS settings because older PCs stored these settings on a CMOS (Complementary Metal Oxide Semiconductor) chip.*

Accessing the CMOS Setup Program

You access the CMOS setup program by pressing the appropriate key or combination of keys during the bootup process. The key used for this purpose varies depending on the manufacturer. For AMI BIOS, use the DELETE key. For Phoenix BIOS, use either F2 or CTRL-ALT-ESC. The exact key or combination of keys is often displayed during bootup, although this message can be disabled. When in doubt, try the DELETE key, F2, or CTRL-ALT-ESC. Alternatively, check the web site of your system manufacturer for more information.

TIP *If you can't get into the CMOS any other way, try holding down as many keys as possible during the boot process. On many systems, this will produce a keyboard error and a message such as "press F1 or F10 to resume."*

CMOS Passwords

The typical CMOS will offer the option to set two passwords—a boot password and a setup password. The boot password must be entered every time the system boots up, and the setup password must be entered in order to enter the CMOS setup program. These passwords provide some security against a casual passerby accessing an unattended PC, but do not secure the PC against intruders with unlimited access to the PC. In the event that you need to clear these passwords, consult your motherboard documentation for information about clearing the CMOS information. Most motherboards provide a jumper that can be set to reset the system to its factory default settings.

TIP Some laptop systems offer an additional password option that encrypts access to the hard drive. These hard drive passwords are more difficult to bypass and are not affected by resetting the CMOS.

TIP On some older systems, the CMOS data relies on a battery that can be removed from the motherboard to clear the BIOS. Removing the battery for several minutes will clear the CMOS data. Most newer systems no longer use these batteries.

Important CMOS Settings

The typical CMOS setup program offers a wide range of options, most of which can safely be left at their default settings.

IDE Device Configuration

For systems with IDE hard drives, use the setup program's IDE autodetect feature to ensure that your IDE drive is properly configured. Instead of detecting the drive and saving its settings, you can simply select AUTO for the drive type. With the AUTO setting, the system will redetect the drives every time the system boots up.

TIP If the CMOS setup program cannot detect the drive, the drive is most likely not properly connected. Double-check the physical connections and confirm that the master/slave settings are properly configured.

Boot Sequence

When installing a new operating system from CD, use the CMOS setup program to configure the system to boot off the CD (if the operating system CD allows for this feature). Typical systems offer options to boot off the floppy, IDE hard drive, or CD-ROM. Some systems provide more advanced options such as specifying a SCSI drive or secondary IDE drive as a boot device.

Integrated Peripherals

Motherboards come with a range of integrated peripherals. Use the CMOS setup program to do the following:

- Configure IRQs and I/O addresses for serial and parallel ports

- Set ECP and EPP modes for parallel ports

- Enable or disable integrated sound and video

CPU Soft Menu

Most motherboards can accept a range of CPUs. Use the CPU Soft Menu to set the bus speed and clock multiplier for the CPU. In many cases, an AUTO option exists that will automatically configure your motherboard for the installed CPU.

CAUTION Some older systems configure these settings using jumpers. Consult your motherboard documentation for the appropriate jumper settings for these motherboards.

Power Management Setup

Power management features can be enabled, disabled, and configured using the CMOS. Current power management schemes require support from the operating system, and specific devices may not work well when power management is enabled. If your system does not wake up cleanly after being suspended, use the CMOS setup program to disable the power management features until you can determine the cause of the problem.

PnP/PCI Configurations

Use the PnP/PCI configuration menu to reserve specific resources (such as IRQs) for your legacy, non-PnP devices.

Fail Safe/Optimized Defaults

Most CMOS setup programs provide two sets of default settings that can be restored: the Fail Safe defaults and the Optimized defaults. The Fail Safe defaults disable many features and typically are used for troubleshooting. Load the Fail Safe defaults and see if the problem goes away. In most instances, the Optimized defaults will be your best bet, enabling most features of the motherboard for maximum stability and performance.

Losing Your CMOS Settings

CMOS settings can be lost for a variety of reasons, including power surges. The loss of CMOS settings can result in various errors during the boot process, such as "CMOS configuration mismatch" or "No boot device available." In most cases, simply reset your configuration to the Optimized Default and reset your hard drive configuration.

If a particular system frequently loses its CMOS settings, consider replacing the onboard battery (if one is present).

Chapter 11

Intel CPUs

Intel Pentium Processor

The original Intel Pentium processor, released in 1993, introduced the 64-bit external data bus common to all current Intel desktop processors. Running at speeds ranging from 60 MHz to 333 MHz and featuring a combination of write-back and write-through caches, Pentium processor- based systems can still be found in many offices. While adequate for basic office tasks, Pentium-based computers cannot provide adequate performance for current operating systems and applications. The features of the Pentium processor are summarized on the next page. Pentium processors were made to fit a variety of sockets, shown in Figure 11-1.

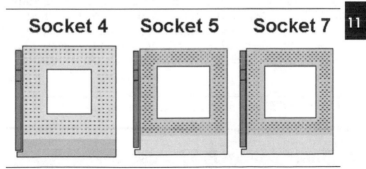

Socket 4   Socket 5   Socket 7

Figure 11-1.   Pentium socket types

TIP When running Pentium-class computers, use applications and operating systems designed to run on that vintage of equipment: Windows 95 or Windows 98. Low-end Pentium processor-based PCs running Linux or BSD can also be used to handle network infrastructure tasks (DNS, mail, firewall, print server) for smaller networks.

Intel Pentium Processor Summary

- **CPU**   Intel Pentium processor
- **Core Speed (MHz)**   60–333
- **External Speed (MHz)**   60–75
- **Clock Multiplier**   1–4.5
- **L1 Cache (KB)**   8WT/8WB or 16WT/16WB
- **L2 Cache**   n/a
- **Internal Voltage**   2.8V, 3.3V, or 5 V
- **External Voltage**   5V or 3.3V
- **Package**   Socket 4, 5, or 7

MMX

In 1996, Intel added MMX support to the Pentium processor. MMX adds to the CPU's instruction set four new registers and 57 new commands that support common multimedia operations. Applications have to be written to specifically take advantage of MMX. AMD and other processor manufacturers also support MMX in their x86-compatible processors.

CAUTION   Not all Pentium processors support MMX.

Intel Pentium Pro Processor

Intel introduced the Pentium Pro processor in 1995. Sometimes referred to as the P6, the Pentium Pro processor built on the foundation of the Pentium processor by adding key additional features, including:

- Quad pipelining
- Dynamic processing
- On-chip L2 cache (either 256KB, 512KB, or 1MB)

The Intel Pentium Pro processor requires a Socket 8 motherboard, as shown in Figure 11-2. The following summarizes the features of the Pentium Pro processor.

Intel Pentium Pro Processor Summary

- **CPU**   Intel Pentium Pro processor
- **Core Speed (MHz)**   166–200
- **External Speed (MHz)**   66
- **Clock Multiplier**   2.5–3
- **L1 Cache (KB)**   8WT/8WB
- **L2 Cache**   256–1024M
- **Internal Voltage**   3.3V
- **External Voltage**   3.1V, 3.3V, or 3.5V
- **Package**   SPGA/Socket 8

Socket 8

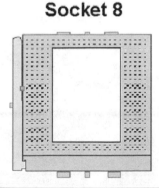

Figure 11-2.   Socket 8, used by Intel Pentium Pro processor

Pentium II Processor

Although running at higher clock speeds, the Pentium II processor provides roughly the same features as the Pentium Pro processor in a new SEC cartridge package. The SEC cartridge fits into a special Slot 1 socket, as shown in Figure 11-3. This summarizes the features of the Pentium II processor:

Intel Pentium II Processor Summary

- **CPU** Intel Pentium II processor
- **Core Speed (MHz)** 233–450
- **External Speed (MHz)** 66–100
- **Clock Multiplier** 3.5–4.5
- **L1 Cache (KB)** 16WT/16WB
- **L2 Cache** 512M
- **Internal Voltage** 2.8V or 2.9V
- **External Voltage** 3.3V
- **Package** SEC Slot 1

Figure 11-3.   Intel Pentium II processor in an SEC cartridge

Pentium III Processor

The Pentium III processor offers incremental improvements over the Pentium II processor, including:

- Support for 100 MHz and 133 MHz motherboards
- Streaming SIMD Extensions (SSE)
- High-speed L2 cache

The features of the Pentium III processor are summarized on the next page.

Used chiefly to speed up graphics applications, SSE adds 70 additional instructions to the CPU's instruction set. The operating system and applications must be written to take advantage of SSE.

NOTE The acronym SIMD stands for Single Instruction/ Multiple Data. MMX, SSE, and SSE2 are all variations on the SIMD concept, which allows the same operation to be performed on multiple pieces of data simultaneously.

Pentium III processors appear in three different packages: the original SECC-2 cartridge (see Figure 11-4) and the newer PPGA (see Figure 11-5) and FC-PGA packages. As always, consult the motherboard documentation to determine the compatibility of a particular processor with a specific motherboard.

11

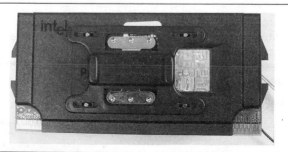

Figure 11-4.   SECC-2 cartridge

Figure 11-5. PPGA package

Pentium III Processor Summary

- **CPU**   Intel Pentium III
- **Core Speed**   450 MHz–1.4 GHz
- **External Speed (MHz)**   100–133
- **Clock Multiplier**   4.5–10.5
- **L1 Cache (KB)**   16WT/16WB
- **L2 Cache**   256–512
- **SSE2**   Yes
- **Core Voltage**   1.7V–2V
- **Package**   SECC-2, PPGA, or FC-PGA

Pentium 4 Processor

The Intel Pentium 4 processor, while fully backward compatible with earlier Pentium processors, represents a radical departure from earlier x86 CPU designs. Intel refers to this new design as the NetBurst micro-architecture. The NetBurst microarchitecture includes:

- Hyper-Threading Technology (3.06 GHz Pentium 4 processor or higher only)
- Hyper-pipelined technology
- 533 MHz or 400 MHz system bus
- Execution trace cache

- Rapid execution engine
- Advanced transfer cache
- Advanced dynamic execution
- Enhanced floating-point and multimedia unit
- Streaming SIMD Extensions 2 (SSE2)

To take full advantage of these enhancements, especially SSE2 and Hyper-Threading Technology, applications must be optimized to use the new microarchitecture. This summarizes the features of the Pentium 4 processor:

Pentium 4 Processor Summary

- **CPU**   Intel Pentium 4
- **Core Speed (GHz)**   1.3–3.06 (expected to approach 10)
- **Front Side Bus (FSB) Speed (MHz)**   400 or 533
- **L2 Cache**   256–512
- **SSE2**   Yes
- **Core Voltage**   1.75V
- **Package**   423-pin PGA or 478-pin PGA

CAUTION   *The performance of applications that have not been optimized for these new features can sometimes suffer. When upgrading to a Pentium 4 processor–based system, consider upgrading to newer versions of your applications that can take advantage of the new features.*

11

Intel Brands

In addition to the Pentium brand, Intel uses three other important brand names for processors: Celeron, Xeon, and Itanium.

Celeron

Intel uses the Intel Celeron brand to designate its economy processors. The original Celeron processor was a "stripped-down" Pentium II without a L2 cache, running at either 266 MHz or 300 MHz. The term "Celeron," however, does not refer to a specific processor. Instead, it has become the Intel moniker for its current low-end desktop processor, whatever that happens to be. Intel has shipped Celeron processors based on the Pentium II, Pentium III, and Pentium 4 cores. Typically, the biggest difference between the premium brand and its Celeron equivalent is the size of the L2 cache.

Xeon

Where Celeron represents an economy option targeted at low-end desktop systems, Intel's Xeon processors target the high-end server market. Like Celeron, Xeon is a brand name that identifies a high-end processor but does not specify a particular chip design. Intel Xeon processors are either Pentium III or Pentium 4 processors featuring special enhancements (chiefly larger L2 caches and motherboard chipsets with special features) that boost server performance.

Itanium

Intel Itanium processors break away from Intel's x86-compatible history and use a completely different architecture: Explicitly Parallel Instruction Computing (EPIC). The Itanium architecture focuses on the needs of data-center servers, providing 64-bit addressing, high-memory bandwidth, and the theoretical ability to scale up to 512 processors in a single server. The Itanium microarchitecture also provides three levels of cache. The current implementation features a 32K L1 cache, a 96K L2 cache, and either a 2MB or 4MB L3 cache.

For more information about current Intel products, consult www.intel.com.

CPUs and Motherboards

Remember, just because the CPU fits into a socket on the motherboard does not mean that the CPU and motherboard are compatible. Always check the documentation (a.k.a the "motherboard book") before installing the CPU, to ensure that the motherboard supports the correct bus speeds, voltages, etc.

Identifying CPU Features

Intel builds a processor ID function into their CPUs. To identify an Intel CPU and determine which features it supports, download Intel's Processor Frequency ID Utility from http://support.intel.com/support/processors/tools/ frequencyid/download.htm.

CAUTION *Manufacturers design motherboards to support specific processors—always consult the motherboard documentation before installing the CPU.*

11

Part II

Operating Systems Technologies

Chapter 12

AMD Processors

AMD (Advanced Micro Devices, Inc.) processors used to be nothing more than clones of equivalent Intel CPUs, but since 1997, AMD has been producing x86-compatible CPUs with additional AMD-specific features and enhancements.

K6 Series

The AMD K6 series processor competed with the Intel Pentium processor. Like the original Pentium, K6 processor-based systems can still be found doing basic computing tasks. While compatible with the Pentium processor's instruction set, the K6 processor included support for a proprietary AMD instruction set, 3DNow!, and provided a larger L1 cache.

3DNow! offered additional SIMD instructions that could enhance the graphics and multimedia performance of applications. Like the MMX instructions with which it competed, applications had to be optimized to take advantage of the 3DNow! instruction set. Table 12-1 summarizes the features of various AMD K6 processors.

TIP   *Low-end K6 processor based PCs running Linux or BSD can often handle network infrastructure tasks (DNS, mail, firewall, print server) for smaller networks.*

Athlon

The AMD Athlon processor has achieved widespread acceptance as a desktop processor. Although AMD's processor designs continue to diverge from Intel's architecture, most applications will run just fine on PCs using either processor.

Gigahertz Equivalency

Originally, AMD named its Athlon processors according to their internal CPU speed. Beginning with the Athlon XP line, AMD began to assign its Athlon processors a "gigahertz equivalency" model number. The AMD Athlon XP 2100+, for example, runs at 1.73 GHz, but AMD claims

CPU	Core Speed (MHz)	External Clock Speed (MHz)	Multi-plier	L1 Cache (KB)	Internal Voltage	External Voltage	Package
AMD K6 processor	66–300	66–100	3–4.5	32WT /32WB	2.2V– 3.2V	3.3V– 3.45V	Super Socket 7
AMD K6-2 processor	450– 550	100	4.5– 5.5	32WT /32WB	2.2V– 2.4V	3.3V	Super Socket 7
AMD K6-III	400– 450	100	4–4.5	32WT /32WB	2.4V	3.3V	Super Socket 7

Table 12-1.   AMD K6 Summary

CPU	Core Speed (MHz)	External Speed (MHz)	Clock Multi-plier	L1 Cache (KB)	L2 Cache	Core Voltage	Package
AMD	500–2250	100–333	5–13.5	64WT/64WB	512M or 256M	1.75V	SEC (Slot A) or CPGA

Table 12-2. AMD Athlon Summary

that, due to architectural features improvements, it provides equivalent performance to the original Athlon running at 2.1 GHz (or 2100 MHz). Look for the + symbol to remind you to distinguish between an Athlon processor's speed in GHz and its gigahertz equivalency model number. The fastest AMD Athlon at the time of this writing, the AMD Athlon XP 2800+, runs at 2250 MHz.

Packages

The original Athlon used a Slot A SEC package (see Figure 12-1). Although this package physically resembles the SEC package used with Slot 1 Intel motherboards, it is not pin-compatible. Newer Athlon processors use a CPGA (Ceramic PGA) package with a 462-pin Socket A (see Figure 12-2).

CAUTION *The original Slot A Athlon will physically fit into a Slot 1 motherboard, but it is not pin-compatible. As always, consult the motherboard documentation to ensure the compatibility of a specific motherboard and CPU combination.*

12

Figure 12-1. Slot A Athlon processor

Figure 12-2. Athlon Socket A

Duron

AMD uses its Duron brand to designate its economy processors. The Duron processors use the same technology as the Athlon but typically have a smaller L2 cache.

Hammer

AMD's Hammer architecture, also known as AMD X86-64, will be its entry into 64-bit computing. To support 64-bit applications, AMD has chosen to extend the x86 instruction set rather than to implement an entirely new architecture as Intel has chosen to do with its Itanium architecture.

For more information about AMD processors, see www.amd.com.

Chapter 13

VIA Processors

VIA produces a line of x86-compatible processors based on technology acquired when it purchased Cyrix in 1999. Rather than competing on performance, the VIA C3 processor fills the niche for a low-cost, low-power CPU alternative for "value" PC systems. The following summarizes the VIA processors. For more information about VIA processors, see www.via.com.tw.

- **CPU**   VIA C3
- **Core Speed**   800–1000 MHz
- **External Speed**   100/133 MHz
- **L1 Cache (KB)**   64WT/64WB
- **L2 Cache**   64
- **Internal Voltage**   1.35V
- **Package**   1.35V   Socket 370

13

Chapter 14

RAM

Adding RAM to Improve Performance

Insufficient RAM (random access memory) is among the most common PC performance issues. When running programs requires more RAM than is physically present, the operating system will swap inactive running programs to available space on the hard drive. Unfortunately, the process of swapping programs back and forth between the RAM and the hard drive slows down the system. The user sees an hourglass and a blinking hard drive activity light. Adding additional RAM may reduce the need to swap programs to the hard drive.

CAUTION *Remember to check your motherboard documentation or the manufacturer's web site before installing RAM. Just because it fits doesn't mean that it's the right RAM for your motherboard.*

RAM Types

RAM comes in a variety of types and packages. As with CPUs, the type of RAM that can be used in a specific system is determined by the motherboard. Consult your motherboard documentation or the manufacturer's web site to determine the appropriate type of RAM for your system.

14

SRAM

Used in cache, SRAM (static RAM) does not need to be refreshed. SRAM has very low latency, making it ideal for use as cache, but its high cost compared to the various types of DRAM makes it unsuitable for use as system RAM.

DRAM

Dynamic RAM consists of memory chips that store 1's and 0's using microscopic capacitors and transistors. DRAM requires periodic refreshing to maintain its stored data.

FPM (Fast Page Mode) RAM

FPM RAM was among the earliest RAM technologies. FPM RAM is obsolete but can still be found in 486 and early Pentium-class computers. FPM RAM comes in 30-pin and 72-pin SIMM (single inline memory module) packages. FPM RAM requires periodic refreshing.

EDO (Extended Data Out) DRAM

EDO RAM requires less frequent refreshing than FMP DRAM, allowing quicker access. EDO was the dominant RAM technology during the 1990s, and can be found in some older PCs, but has been replaced by SDRAM in most new systems. It is typically found in 72-pin SIMM and 168-pin DIMM (dual inline memory module) packages.

SDRAM (Synchronous DRAM)

SDRAM runs synchronously with the system clock, meaning that it runs at the same speed as other components, such as the CPU and the chipset. SDRAM is available in five clock speeds: 66 MHz, 75 MHz, 83 MHz, 100 MHz, and 133 MHz. SDRAM typically is found in 168-pin DIMM, 72-pin SO-DIMM, or 144-pin SO-DIMM packages. The SO-DIMM (small outline DIMM) package is generally found in notebook computers.

PC100/133 SDRAM

PC100 and PC133 RAM (running at 100 MHz and 133 MHZ, respectively) is SDRAM that includes an additional serial presence detect (SPD) chip that communicates information about the RAM to the motherboard to ensure proper operation. Most motherboards that use SDRAM today require PC100 or PC133 SDRAM. SDRAM typically comes in 168-pin DIMM packages.

DDR SDRAM (Double Data Rate SDRAM)

DDR SDRAM doubles the throughput of regular SDRAM by allowing two accesses for every clock cycle. DDR SDRAM comes in 184-pin DIMM packages and runs at either 200 MHz or 266 MHz.

RDRAM (Rambus DRAM)

RDRAM provides high-speed RAM capable of running at speeds of up to 800 MHz and supporting throughput of up to 1.6 GHz. RDRAM is less common than DDR SDRAM because of its high cost. Rambus is rarely found in desktop PCs because of its high cost.

Error-Checking RAM

While today's RAM chips provide sufficient reliability for most uses, in mission-critical applications such as network servers you will often find error-checking RAM using one of two technologies: parity or ECC. Parity RAM, typically found in SIMMs, adds an extra bit for every byte that the system can use to check for errors. ECC (error correction code) RAM, typically found in DIMMs, uses a more sophisticated error-checking mechanism for the same purpose. As always, consult your motherboard documentation to see if your system requires parity or ECC RAM.

14

Banking

When adding RAM, the RAM chips must be added in complete banks. A *bank* of RAM consists of enough RAM packages to match the width of the external data bus of the CPU, which is 64 bits on all CPUs since the introduction of the Intel Pentium processor (see Table 14-1). Each stick of RAM within a bank must be identical in terms of RAM type and speed.

TIP   *The magic banking formula is:*
One bank = width of the external data bus ÷ width of the SIMM or DIMM.

Package	Width
30-pin SIMM	8 bits
72-pin SIMM	32 bits
168-pin DIMM	64 bits
72-pin SO-DIMM	32 bits
144-pin SO-DIMM	64 bits

Table 14-1.   Width-of-RAM Reference Chart

Chapter 15

IDE Hard Drives

Integrated Drive Electronics (IDE) drives dominate the market for desktop PCs. Sometimes referred to as ATA drives, IDE drives provide a cost-effective means for adding mass storage to a stand-alone PC.

CAUTION The term IDE can accurately be used to describe both ATA drives and SCSI drives, because all current hard drives use integrated controllers (hence, Integrated Drive Electronics). However, in practice, the term IDE almost always refers to ATA drives. The only place you will find the "IDE nature" of SCSI drives discussed is in highly technical discussions of the internals of hard drive technology. If you see the term IDE on a box, advertisement, or instruction sheet, you can confidently assume that the IDE drive is an ATA drive.

IDE Size Limitations

The history of IDE technology has been marked by ever-increasing limitations on size. To support drives over certain limits, both the hard drive and the hard drive controller must support the appropriate standards. The current standard for 48-bit addressing supports drives with a theoretical capacity of 144 petabytes (144,115,188,075,855,360 bytes) and will hopefully provide sufficient capacity for the foreseeable future (but we've all heard that before!). Eventually, 48-bit addressing support will become part of the upcoming ATA/ATAPI 6 standard, but until that standard becomes finalized by the ANSI T13 committee, drives and controllers supporting 48-bit addressing will be sold under a variety of names, such as Maxtor's "Big Drives" support. Until the standard is finalized, consult your hard drive and drive controller documentation to determine support for disks larger than

15

137GB. Consult www.t13.org for the latest information about upcoming ATA/ATAPI standards. Table 15-1 also provides recommendations for large drives and the support they require.

TIP *If your current PC does not support larger disks, several companies make add-on IDE controllers that support the latest standards. These add-on cards can be used either to supplement or replace the motherboard's onboard IDE controller.*

IDE Speeds

IDE speeds have been increasing for PIO modes, DMA, and Ultra ATA/66/100/133. All of these technologies require support from both the hard drive and the IDE controller. In most cases, a faster drive used with a controller that doesn't support its full operation will function at the highest speed that both support.

Installation

IDE drives connect to a 40-pin connector using a 40-pin ribbon cable. To support higher-speed, ATA/66 and ATA/100 devices use the new 40-pin, 80-wire cable (see Figure 15-1). For power, IDE drives use the standard Molex connector.

Drives Bigger Than	Require Support For
504MB	LBA (logical block addressing) or ECHS (enhanced CHS)
8.4GB	INT 13h extensions (Interrupt 13)
137GB	48-bit addressing support

Table 15-1. Hard Drive Size Support Guide

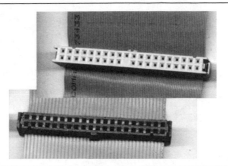

Figure 15-1   80-wire and 40-wire IDE cables both use a
40 pin connector.

A typical system will have two IDE controllers, typically
referred to as the primary and secondary controllers.
Each controller can support up to two devices.

To enable the system to distinguish between the devices,
the first drive should be set to master and the second
drive to slave. The position on the cable is not important—
the setting, usually determined by jumpers, determines
the drive's status as master or slave. Some drives also
have a "1 drive" or "single drive" setting for use when
no slave drive is present. Most drives have the master/slave
settings clearly labeled, as shown in Figure 15-2.

TIP   *The best way to know if your drive is properly
configured is to run the CMOS setup program's autodetect
feature. If the autodetect function finds all the drives in
the system, the drive is properly connected, and the
master and slave settings have been properly configured.
If the drive does not show up for the autodetect feature,
double-check your physical connections, including the
Molex power connector, and confirm the master and slave
drive settings.*

TIP   *Pin 1 on the ribbon cable is typically marked with
a colored stripe. Use that stripe and the markings on the
controller to make certain that you are not reversing
the cable.*

15

Figure 15-2. Drive label showing master/slave settings

NOTE *Some newer systems use rounded IDE cables to improve airflow inside the PC case. These cables are functionally equivalent to the traditional ribbon cables.*

Chapter 16

EIDE Devices

Enhanced IDE (EIDE) can support other types of mass storage devices in addition to hard drives. Common mass storage IDE devices include:

- CD-ROM drives
- CD-RW drives
- Zip and other removable media drives
- DVD drives

EIDE mass storage devices use the same 40-pin cabling and master/slave settings as IDE hard drives.

Performance

Although EIDE mass storage devices and hard drives can share the same controller, to maintain optimal system performance, you should install slower devices on a different IDE controller. For example, install your hard drives on the primary controller and your CD-ROM and DVD drives on the secondary controller.

CAUTION *Installing faster and slower IDE devices on the same controller can force the faster device to operate at a slower speed to maintain compatibility.*

SCSI vs. IDE

For many years, SCSI (Small Computer System Interface) devices held a decisive advantage over IDE devices in terms of performance and expandability. The introduction of higher performance standards for IDE devices and the widespread availability of add-on cards with additional

IDE controllers have narrowed the gap between SCSI
and IDE in terms of both performance and expandability.
In environments such as network servers, where multiple
devices are likely to be accessed simultaneously, SCSI
continues to enjoy a performance advantage. In the
typical desktop system, however, IDE provides similar
performance at a lower cost.

Chapter 17

CMOS Settings
for IDE Devices

Detection

IDE devices can be detected using the CMOS setup
program's autodetect feature. This autodetect feature
is your best method to confirm the proper physical
installation of an IDE device. If autodetection fails,
check all master/slave settings, as well as power and
data cable connections.

On current systems, you can configure the system to
automatically detect IDE devices each time the system
boots. This configuration will work for most systems but
will slow the boot process, because the system must wait
for nonexistent devices to time out.

Mode Support

While many IDE devices can automatically configure
themselves to support enhanced features such as PIO
modes, on some older systems, you may have to configure
these settings manually. Consult your motherboard or
controller card documentation for more information.

Driver Support

Note that while removable media devices (CD-ROM, tape
drive, and so on) will be detected by most BIOS versions,
the BIOS usually does not provide support for these
devices. The BIOS merely reports whatever identification

17

information the manufacturer chooses to program into the device. To make these devices work, you must install the appropriate driver for your operating system.

On older systems, you sometimes are offered a choice of LBA, Normal, or Large when autodetecting hard drives. The LBA and Large settings refer to two slightly different methods of supporting hard drives larger than 504MB. Note that these older systems are limited to hard drives smaller than 8.4GB—for larger drives, you need to upgrade to a motherboard or controller that supports interrupt 13h (INT 13h) extensions (up to 137GB) or 48-bit addressing (>137GB).

NOTE *Sometimes, the original size limitation for IDE is listed as 528 million bytes instead of 504 megabytes. Remember that a megabyte is equal to 1,058,576 bytes— the expressions 528 million bytes and 504 megabytes are equivalent. Unfortunately, hard drive manufacturers often use "millions of bytes," and the rest of the industry tends to use "megabytes." This leads to some confusion when the two different notations appear in the same documentation.*

Chapter 18

Partitioning and Formatting

A partition is a logical division of the hard drive. A blank hard drive cannot be used to store data until it has been organized into partitions.

A hard disk may have from one to four partitions. While many systems use a single partition, creating multiple partitions offers several advantages:

- Enabling multiple operating systems to be booted on the same PC

- Overcoming operating system limitations on the maximum size of a partition

- Simplifying recovery of data following catastrophic system failures

- Simplifying data migration between systems

These advantages do not apply to every system—most single-user desktop systems do fine with one partition per hard disk.

There are two types of partitions: primary and extended. The key distinction between primary and extended partitions is that primary partitions can hold an operating system, whereas extended partitions can be further divided into multiple logical drives.

TIP   The tools that come with the various versions of Microsoft Windows tend to limit the types of partitions you can create. To create multiple primary partitions, for example, you need either a third-party product, such as Partition Magic, or the disk partition tools from another operating system, such as Linux.

TIP   Windows 2000 and Windows XP did not initially support partitions larger than 137GB. To support larger partitions, download the latest system updates from www.microsoft.com.

Partitioning Tools

To create partitions, you use either FDISK (for DOS or Windows 95/98/Me/NT) or the Disk Management extension (for Windows 2000 and Windows XP). FDISK is a command-line utility, generally run from a bootable floppy disk. The Disk Management extension is an integrated part of the graphical Microsoft Management Console (MMC), and can be found in the Control Panel by selecting Administrative Tools | Computer Management | Disk Management (shown in Figure 18-1).

CAUTION   *Repartitioning a drive will destroy any data previously stored on the drive!*

TIP   *With Windows 2000 and Windows XP, you may wish to limit your partitions to less than 137GB even if the Disk Administrator program allows you to create a single partition larger than 137GB. Unpatched versions of Windows 2000 and Windows XP cannot recognize partitions larger than 137GB, making it difficult to reinstall the operating system to a drive containing a single partition over 137GB. Your original partition (and its data!) may be lost if you ever need to reinstall the operating system and cannot find or create a prepatched installation CD, so be sure to back up often!*

Active Partition

Although a system can theoretically have up to four primary partitions, only one partition can be set as "active." The active partition holds the operating system that the system will launch during the boot process. Set the active partition using the same tool that you use to create partitions: FDISK for Windows 95/98/Me/NT and the Disk Management extension for Windows 2000 or XP.

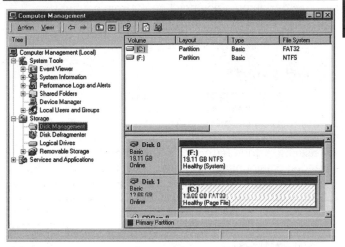

Figure 18-1. The Windows 2000 Disk Management extension

CAUTION *If you fail to set an active partition, the system will not boot even if the operating system itself is properly installed.*

TIP *By default, the Windows Setup program for Windows 95/98/Me/NT, Windows 2000, and Windows XP will create a single primary partition and make it active. Multiple partitions are not required.*

Extended Partitions and Logical Drives

In addition to primary partitions, a system may have extended partitions. An extended partition cannot contain a bootable operating system, but can be further divided into one or more logical drives.

In general, most modern single-user desktop systems use a single partition per hard drive. While smaller logical drives reduced wasted space when using the older FAT16 file system, modern systems using the FAT32 or NTFS file systems derive no efficiency benefit from having their hard drives broken into multiple logical drives.

Drive Letters

Microsoft Windows assigns a drive letter to each primary partition or logical drive. In Windows 95/98/Me/NT, drive letters are assigned automatically. Primary partitions are assigned drive letters first, then logical drives in the extended partitions. In Windows 2000 and XP, the default drive letter assignments work the same way, but can be modified using the Disk Management extension.

Formatting

Partitioning divides the drives into large divisions of disk space, but those divisions must be organized for use by formatting each partition. In Windows 95/98/Me/NT, use the FORMAT command. In Windows 2000 or XP, use the Disk Management extension. Formatting creates a structure for storing and retrieving files from the drive. The exact structure will vary depending on the file system used. Windows 95/98/Me/NT systems use FAT16 or FAT32, while Windows 2000 or XP systems use NTFS.

TIP *Windows 2000 and XP both support FAT32 in addition to NTFS, but the only reason to use FAT32 would be to make files on the partition available to another operating system on a dual-boot system.*

Chapter 19

SCSI Fundamentals

Fundamentals of SCSI

The Small Computer Systems Interface (SCSI) began as a way to configure mass storage that was not dependent on the operating system involved. Although SCSI technology can be found in numerous types of devices, its primary function is for storage devices including hard drives, tape drives, and CD-ROMs.

Components of SCSI

The following are the components and functions of SCSI:

- **Host adapter card**   Typically has an external connector for beginning the SCSI chain (daisy-chained SCSI devices) and an internal connector for connecting to the internal PC system (see Figure 19-1).

- **SCSI ID**   All devices communicate with the adapter card using an ID number. This number can range from 0–7 for older SCSI configurations and 0–15 for new SCSI standards. Remember that the lower the number, the higher the priority of the device; a device with SCSI ID 6 has lower priority than a device with SCSI ID 2. Devices cannot share a SCSI ID. The host adapter is generally set at SCSI ID 7. ID numbers are typically set by a jumper or a switch.

- **Termination**   A signal traveling down the SCSI cable will bounce back when it reaches the end of the wire if it is not properly terminated. A terminator absorbs the signal and prevents "bounce-back." Many SCSI devices have a terminator built in (see Figure 19-2); a device that is the last in the chain must have the terminator plugged in or be set to self-terminate.

Figure 19-1. SCSI host adaptor

SCSI Types

Over time, SCSI has been upgraded and a variety of standards have developed. The following are the major standards and descriptions:

- **SCSI-1** This standard is defined by an 8-bit/5-MHz bus and can support up to eight devices. Because it was the first standard, the rules were a bit looser, and not all SCSI-1 devices worked well together.

- **SCSI-2** This standard was described in more detail to reduce the chance of device incompatibility. SCSI-2

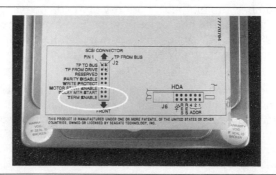

Figure 19-2. Some devices can be set to terminate using a jumper.

also added a common command set (CCS), a set of commands that all SCSI-2 devices must use. This standard used an 8-bit data transfer rate, but it could be set to a 5-MHz or 10-MHz bus speed (called Fast SCSI). Another variety of SCSI-2, called Wide SCSI, allowed 16-bit bus widths, and a 32-bit bus width was also later added. High cost kept SCSI-2 from becoming widely accepted early on.

19

- **SCSI-3** The main improvement of SCSI-3 (with added names like Ultra, Ultra2, and Wide Ultra) is that is allows up to 16 devices in a chain. Still using an 8- or 16-bit bus width, the speeds have increased, allowing up to an 80-MHz bus speed. Ultra SCSI (20 MHz), Ultra2 SCSI (40 MHz), and Ultra3 SCSI (80 MHz) fall into Narrow (8-bit) or Wide (16-bit) bus widths.

A summary of the SCSI types, speeds, and number of devices supported can be found in Table 19-1.

Internal and External SCSI Devices

As mentioned earlier, SCSI devices can be connected externally or internally. The only difference lies in the type of cabling used to connect the devices to the host adapter card. The following are the types of SCSI cables used:

- **Type A SCSI cable** 50 wires, 8-bit data transfer; used by SCSI-1 and SCSI-2 and 8-bit Fast SCSI-2 (see Figure 19-3).

- **Type B SCSI cable** Not widely used anymore, this allowed 16-bit data transfer and was used in parallel with a Type A cable.

- **Type P SCSI cable** Replaced Type B; has 68 wires and can be used without a Type A cable in parallel.

- **SCA 80 SCSI cable** 80-pin cable used by faster SCSI-3 devices. SCSI-3 can also use 68-wire cables.

SCSI Trade Assoc. Terms	Bus Speed (MB/s)	Bus Width (bits)	Max. Bus Lengths Meters[1]			Max. Device Support
			SE	LVD	HVD	
SCSI-1[2]	5	8	6 [3]	25		8
Fast SCSI-1[2]	10	8	3 [3]	25		8
Fast Wide SCSI	20	16	3 [3]	25		16
Ultra SCSI[2]	20	8	1.5 [3]	25		8
Ultra SCSI[2]	20	8	3	-	-	4
Wide Ultra SCSI	40	16	- [3]	25		16
Wide Ultra SCSI	40	16	1.5	-	-	8
Wide Ultra SCSI	40	16	3	-	-	4
Ultra2 SCSI[2,4]	40	8	[4]	12	25	8
Wide Ultra2 SCSI[4]	80	16	[4]	12	25	16
Ultra3 SCSI or Ultra160[6]	160	16	[4]	12	[5]	16
Ultra320	320	16	[4]	12	[5]	16

(Table courtesy of the SCSI Trade Association—http://www.scita.org)

Table 19-1. SCSI Types

External SCSI Connectors

External connectors for SCSI come in a variety of shapes and are always female. The types include:

- 50-pin Centronics–obsolete SCSI-1 connector
- 50-pin HD SCSI-2
- 68-pin HD DB, used for SCSI-2 and SCSI-3
- 25-pin D-type (similar to parallel connector) used for SCSI-2 and some removable drives

Figure 19-3. Type A SCSI cable

Chapter 20

SCSI Installation, Cabling, and Troubleshooting

20

Installing and Configuring SCSI Devices

Plug and Play technology has made installing SCSI devices extremely simple. Most versions of the Windows operating system have a built-in set of drivers for communicating with SCSI adapter cards and devices.

Steps to Install

The first step involves installing the SCSI Host Adapter Card. Adaptec is a common manufacturer to look for, and you'll find a variety of PCI SCSI cards that comply with the Hardware Compatibility List. Install the card using the instructions provided with the card, and, if necessary, install the device driver when prompted. Windows 9x and above usually recognize most SCSI cards.

Be sure to match the SCSI card with the type of devices to which you will connect it. Buying Wide SCSI devices will do you no good without a Wide SCSI controller card. When installing the card, take notes on the SCSI ID numbers you will be using, and remember to terminate the host adapter if it's the end of the external chain (or the internal chain). Most Adaptec adapters are self-terminating and will autodetect whether they are on the end of the chain.

Resolving SCSI ID Conflicts

The final word of caution involves the SCSI ID numbers. Most of the good SCSI adapter cards come with software that helps you troubleshoot any problems. The easiest and quickest solution, however, is to visibly check all devices and verify that the SCSI ID numbers that are set are valid for the device and are not duplicated by any other device. Remember that some devices cannot use a particular SCSI ID number, so check documentation on all devices for this type of information.

If two devices are sharing an ID number, the software usually informs you in a not so subtle way. One typical scenario that happens when an ID number has been duplicated is that the software reports that *all* devices have the same ID number. It's up to you to determine which devices are sharing an ID number.

Chapter 21

I/O Addresses

Input/Output Addresses

When the CPU addresses programs and hardware, it needs
to know how to differentiate between the external data
bus and the address bus. The peripherals and programs
that will communicate with the CPU need to know when
the CPU is talking directly to them.

How It Happens

Starting with the 8086 CPU, an extra wire was added
to the bus so that hardware devices could differentiate
between the CPU sending a signal to a memory address
versus a device. When this IO/MEM (input/output or
memory) wire is turned on (meaning voltage is flowing
through it), the RAM memory ignores the other signals
on the bus, and all devices listen for a specific pattern
of 1s and 0s, which determine to which device the CPU
is sending.

Sixteen bits of data are used to specify this pattern of 1s
and 0s. The variation of the pattern is quite large, but
the number of devices contained within a PC is limited.
Therefore, each device listens to a grouping of numbers
on the address bus. These collections of numbers make up
what is called the I/O addresses of the device. Table 21-1
contains a listing of example I/O addresses.

Addressing

Addressing in I/O is actually in binary but is typically
expressed in hexadecimal. An I/O address of
0000001111110000 represents the start of the floppy
drive grouping, but in hex this is represented as 03F0.

I/O Address Range	Usage
0000-000F	DMA controller
0020-002F	Master IRQ controller
0030-003F	Master IRQ controller
0040-0043	System timer
0060-0063	Keyboard
0070-0071	CMOS clock
0080-008F	DMA page registers
0090-009F	DMA page resisters
00A0-00AF	Slave IRQ controller
00B0-OOBF	Slave IRQ controller
00C0-00CF	DMA controller
00E0-00EF	Reserved
00F0-00FF	Math coprocessor
0170-0177	Secondary hard drive controller
01F0-01FF	Primary hard drive controller
0200-0207	Joystick
0210-0217	Reserved
0278-027F	LPT2
02B0-02DF	Secondary EGA
02E8-02EF	COM4
02F8-02FF	COM2
0378-037F	LPT1
03B0-03BF	Mono video
03C0-03CF	Primary EGA
03D0-03DF	CGA video
03E8-03EF	COM3
03F0-03F7	Floppy controller
03F8-03FF	COM1

Table 21-1. The Original I/O Addresses and Devices Listening for Them

There are devices in existence today (network cards and sound cards, for example) that do not have a reserved I/O address range. These can use reserved I/O ranges between 0210 and 0278. Also, the last I/O address range specified is 03FF, but there is nothing to prevent a device from using a higher hexadecimal range.

Rules of I/O

There are three rules for I/O addressing:

- All devices in a PC will have I/O addresses.
- All devices in a PC will use more than one I/O address.
- An assigned I/O address cannot be used by any other device.

21

Chapter 22

IRQs

IRQs

You know how the CPU uses I/O addressing for two-way communication with a device, but how does a device let the processor know when it needs CPU time? The process is called *interruption,* and the processors in a PC have a wire (called INT) that signals the CPU when a device wishes to communicate. What happens when multiple devices all wish to talk to the CPU at the same time? A simple matter of 15 wires called IRQs (Interrupt Requests) solves the problem.

The Rules

When it comes to IRQs, there is a short list of rules to obey:

- Every device needs an IRQ assigned to it, including devices built into the motherboard.

- No two devices can share an IRQ.

- If two devices are using the same IRQ, the system will experience problems (now or later).

New PCs and operating systems now use Plug and Play (discussed in Chapter 24) to handle the assignments of IRQs, but before Plug and Play evolved into what it is today, devices had to be manually assigned an IRQ (via a jumper or software). There are 15 IRQs, most of which have been assigned and accepted as "standards" by the manufacturing community (see Table 22-1 for a listing). For example, if your company makes keyboards, you design those devices to use IRQ1. Using IRQ6 would be a bad idea, as the floppy drive manufacturers use IRQ6 as their default.

IRQ	Default Function
IRQ 0	System timer
IRQ 1	Keyboard
IRQ 2/9	Open for use (PCI steering)
IRQ 3	Default COM2, COM4
IRQ 4	Default COM1, COM3
IRQ 5	LPT2 (sound cards)
IRQ 6	Floppy drive
IRQ 7	LPTI
IRQ 8	Real-time clock
IRQ 10	Open for use
IRQ 11	Open for use (USB)
IRQ 12	Open for use (PS/2 mouse port)
IRQ 13	Math coprocessor
IRQ 14	Primary hard drive controller
IRQ 15	Secondary hard drive controller

Table 22-1. IRQ Assignments

There are some open IRQs that Plug and Play systems will attempt to use if they are found to be unused. USB tends to take control of IRQ11. Just keep in mind that unused IRQs will find a device to use them eventually.

COM and LPT

When PCs began growing in popularity, IBM created a way of grouping IRQs and I/O addresses together. These groups were very useful for devices using two-way communication (modems come to mind) and were given the name COM ports. Printers also found a use for a grouping called LPT ports. Table 2-22 lists the I/O addresses and IRQs for some popular COM and LPT ports.

Port	I/O Address	IRQ
COM1	3F8	4
COM2	2F8	3
LPT1	378	7
LPT2	278	5
COM3	3E8	4
COM4	2E8	3

Table 22-2. COM and LPT Combinations

By using a COM or LPT port, the process of selecting IRQ and I/O addresses is simplified. Note that some ports are using the same IRQ. In older PCs, this was allowed, but in newer PCs, it causes the PC to lock up. Plug and Play helps to solve this issue.

Chapter 23

DMA

Direct Memory Access

CPUs are the busiest device in a PC. They perform calculations for hardware, software, and the operating system. They listen for IRQs and move data in and out of memory constantly. With all this work going on, the CPU became both the brains of the PC and the gateway to the memory. A new technology was developed to take some of the load off the CPU. Direct Memory Access (DMA) allows certain devices to communicate directly with memory, freeing up a little of the CPU's precious time.

How It Works

DMA allows certain devices to talk directly with RAM. DMA occurs using an IBM 8237 chip included on the motherboard. A wire sends a signal to the processor indicating that a device wishes to communicate directly with the external data bus. The path for this signal is known as a DMA channel. Eight channels are available (see Table 23-1), which means eight different possible devices can use DMA. Most of the DMA channels are not assigned, however, which enables manufacturers to create hardware that can use DMA.

Just as with IRQs, when a device wishes to use DMA, it sends a signal on one of the DMA channels. No two devices can share a DMA channel.

Limitations

Initially, DMA was designed for ISA standards; therefore, DMA was limited to an 8 MHz bus speed. Even though current DMA uses 16-bit data transfer, the speed limitation

DMA Channel	Type	Function
0	8-bit	None
1	8-bit	Open for use
2	8-bit	Floppy drive controller
3	8-bit	Open for use
5	16-bit	Open for use
6	16-bit	Open for use
7	16-bit	Open for use

Table 23-1. DMA assignments

is still there. For newer PCs, DMA just wasn't fast enough, but a new procedure called bus mastering has kept DMA alive.

Bus Mastering

Hard drives that communicate directly with the external data bus use bus mastering, which skips the DMA chipset and simply watches the external data bus for periods of activity. When it detects activity on the bus, it simply "turns off" the device's ability to talk directly for a period of time—this saves CPU time and increases availability of the CPU for other activities. Bus mastering allows some of todays faster drives to use DMA-type access to increase the speeds of PCs and servers. The most current standard (and the one widely accepted as the industry standard) is Ultra DMA.

Chapter 24

Plug and Play

Plug and Play

Plug and Play is supposed to be the answer to simple PC device configuration. Sometimes it doesn't quite work the way it's supposed to, but those moments are becoming more rare with every new operating system and hardware device released.

How It Works

24⁻

First, for Plug and Play (PnP) to work properly, you have to have a PnP-compatible BIOS. Older BIOS may not recognize the PnP capabilities of the devices installed. Second, the operating system has to support PnP. Windows 98 and higher will work with PnP (the exceptions being Windows NT 3.0 and higher and Windows 95, but you can download upgrades to add that functionality). And third, you need devices that are PnP compliant. All new devices these days are PnP compliant. If you find a device that isn't PnP, buy something else.

When in doubt, remember that most PCI devices (99 percent) are PnP compatible. ISA devices are questionable and, if possible, should be replaced with PCI devices anyway. ISA is an older technology that you should attempt to replace with PCI; the hardware is slower and does not support PnP.

If you have satisfied these three requirements, on bootup, any new PnP-compliant device will be detected first by the BIOS and then by the operating system. PnP first assigns IRQs to any legacy devices (non-PnP) and then assigns an IRQ to PnP devices. BIOS asks every PnP device what resources it needs and assigns them automatically. Certain devices can only use specific IRQs, and BIOS attempts to satisfy all the hardware requests. One of the nice features of PnP is the ability to reassign resources that a PnP device uses. This is done from within the operating system. If all legacy and PnP devices are working well with BIOS, the operating system boots normally and receives the device configuration information from BIOS. Device drivers may still need to be installed for Windows to communicate effectively with a new device. Any problems can also be resolved from within the operating system.

Chapter 25

Printer Connections, Modes, and Troubleshooting

Printer Connections and Troubleshooting

The variety of printers available today is huge, but the methods for connecting them to a PC are still few. This chapter discusses the most common methods for connecting printers to a PC.

Serial Printers

First, don't ever buy a printer that only connects via a serial port; they're almost impossible to find, but the day may come when you'll find one. Using a DB-9 or DB-25 connector, these old printers connect to the back of a PC and are extremely slow and out of date.

Parallel Port Printers

Although parallel port printers are still the most common type, they are quickly being replaced by USB. However, a printer that connects via a parallel port is still fairly fast and transfers data at a rate of about 150 kilobytes per second.

USB Port Printers

The USB port provides printers with a faster connection than the parallel port. USB 1.0 and 2.0 both support printers, but when purchasing a printer that uses USB 2.0, be sure that your PC also supports USB 2.0, to gain the maximum speed from the printer; in some instances, the printer may work, just at a slower speed, and in other instances, it won't work at all. Other than performance, one other advantage with USB printers is the ability to plug and unplug them to and from the PC without having to power down the PC.

IEEE 1284

With many types of printers, there are certain standards for how the printers communicate with the PC. The Institute of Electrical and Electronics Engineers (IEEE) organization, an international group that sets standards for technology, defined a standard in 1991 to help manufacturers build printers that were more reliable and easier to manage.

Basically, the IEEE 1284 standard requires compliant printers to support the following:

- Five modes of operation (Compatibility, Nibble mode, Byte mode, EPP, and ECP)

- A standard negotiation method for helping PCs and printers to determine which modes are supported when connected

- A standard physical connection

- A standard electrical connection

Troubleshooting Common Printer Issues

When troubleshooting printers, the list of common problems include the following:

- **Problems with feed mechanisms**   Check to make sure there isn't too much paper loaded. Also check to make sure paper is loaded and properly seated in the tray.

- **Problems with tractor feeds**   Check that holes line up exactly with tractor feeds. Make sure paper is threaded completely on the feeds to ensure proper alignment.

- **Out of Paper error**   Add paper to the printer.

- **Input/Output errors** Make sure the printer is plugged in, powered up, and connected using proper cables. Check that the proper driver is installed and that IRQ and I/O settings are correct for legacy printers.

- **No Default Printer error** Either a printer isn't installed or a specific printer is expected to be the default printer for an application. Check that the correct printer is set to default.

- **Toner/Ink low** Check that toner/ink cartridges are actually installed. Take them out, shake them, and then reinsert them. If this doesn't work, replace the cartridges.

- **Paper jam** Read the documentation to know exactly what can and cannot be opened. Open all access points to the printer and clear paper stuck in the printer.

- **Dot-matrix print quality is poor** This can happen for different reasons, but can include dirty printheads, incorrect paper type, and old ribbons.

- **Inkjet print quality is poor** Check that ink cartridges are full and not too old. Clogged nozzles are a thing of the past with newer inkjets, but with older printers, the nozzles may need to be cleaned.

- **Laser print quality is poor** Usually this indicates low toner, but it is possible the drum isn't discharging properly. Laser printer repairs should be done by a qualified technician. Light and dark printing problems can usually be attributed to faulty hardware, such as the drum. Removing and shaking the toner cartridge might get you a few extra uses out of it, but replacing the cartridge might also fix faded print jobs. Wrinkled or reused paper can also cause problems, as can dirty rollers in the printer.

Cleaning

It's important to clean your printers. Below is a list of the common areas to clean for each type of printer:

- **Dot-matrix** Use compressed air to clean dust and debris from the printer. Replace the ribbon

25

if necessary. Clean the printhead with denatured alcohol. Replace the carriage belt if it shows signs of wear or is loose.

- **Inkjet** Remove ink cartridge(s). Blow out dust and debris with compressed air. Wipe off ink cartridge nozzles with a damp cloth. Wipe away any ink found inside the printer. Replace the carriage belt if it's loose or worn.

- **Laser** Remove and clean off the toner cartridge. Use compressed air to clean out dust and debris. Use denatured alcohol to clean the transfer corona. Clean fusing rollers and replace roller pads and the ozone filter. Clean the rubber guide rollers with water.

Chapter 26

Power Management

Power Management for Portable Computers

Laptops can use standard AC power, but it is the ability to run off of a battery that makes portable PCs possible. Batteries have a limited power life, though, so power management has become an important issue with portables.

System Management Mode

System Management Mode (SMM) gives control to the CPU to slow down or stop its internal clock, thus saving power. In order to use SMM, the portable has to have a compatible BIOS as well as an operating system capable of communicating with and understanding the requests SMM is making of the hardware. SMM was eventually replaced with APM and ACPI, due mainly to the fact that in a portable, it isn't always the CPU that needs to be able to limit power usage. You may still encounter some older systems that use SMM, but if you're purchasing a new portable, look for APM/ACPI support instead of SMM.

APM/ACPI

Advanced Power Management (APM) was implemented shortly after SMM, and added some functionality to SMM:

- **Full On** The system is running at full power consumption and power management is disabled or not built in.

- **APM Enabled** The CPU and memory will run at full power, but other devices (if designed to support APM) may be able to be shut down to reduce power usage.

101

- **APM Standby**   The CPU is stopped. Memory still uses power to maintain any information stored. Other hardware is shut down, but configuration settings are saved in memory.

- **APM Suspend**   The portable will run at its lowest power consumption and all devices are powered down. When suspending, or hibernating, a system, the current system's configuration (including memory and programs currently running) is written to the hard drive. When the system is awakened, the information is written from the hard drive back into memory.

- **Off**   System is completely down and no system settings are saved to the hard drive or to memory. Power usage does not occur.

Advanced Configuration and Power Interface (ACPI) has the same functionality as APM along with some other features. A popular one is the Soft Power On/Off, which allows the Power button on a desktop or portable to be set to a particular APM setting. Instead of completely turning off a PC, the Power button could be programmed to send the PC into hibernation or standby mode.

Configuring APM/ACPI

Some settings are configured using the CMOS Setup Utility, and others are defined from within the operating system. If APM/ACPI functionality is important, be certain to verify that the BIOS supports APM or ACPI. A Windows PC may be able to control some aspects of the hardware power consumption, but without support from the BIOS, these controls may be extremely limited or nonexistent.

Chapter 27

USB and FireWire

USB and FireWire in Portables

Desktops and servers have benefited from the new bus standards: USB and IEEE 1394 (FireWire). Portable PCs are also finding the new standards useful

USB

Universal Serial Bus (USB) is standard equipment on most new PCs, servers, and portables. Supporting up to 127 devices, USB does not require the operating system to reboot in order to use the USB hardware. Simply plug the device in, install any drivers required, and begin to use the device.

USB version 1.1 runs at one of two speeds: 1.5 Mbps (for devices like the mouse) or 12 Mbps (for external drives, for example). Version 2.0 is capable of supporting speeds up to 480 Mbps.

USB devices are limited to a five meter cable length, but this can be extended by using a powered USB hub. Keep in mind that the shorter the cable, the less electrical interference will typically be encountered.

27

NOTE *Always make sure that USB is supported in CMOS. An IRQ must be designated for each USB port. Also, Windows 95A and Windows NT are the only operating systems that do not support USB "out of the box." For these two operating systems, you must download a USB supplement from the Microsoft web site in order to support USB devices.*

FireWire

USB is fast, but new technologies such as digital cameras and digital video are placing speed demands even on USB version 2.0. In 1995, the IEEE released standard 1394, also called FireWire. FireWire provides a bidirectional, high-speed cabling solution to connect new devices to desktops, servers, and portable devices.

FireWire uses a special 6-pin cable. It has a unique shape, just like USB, and will only fit in a FireWire port. It provides power and data transfer. There is also a 4-pin FireWire cable, but it does not supply power to a device.

FireWire can run at speeds of 100, 200, and 400 Mbps. Portable devices typically do not come with FireWire ports, however, so adding a FireWire PC Card is almost always required.

And finally, FireWire supports up to 63 devices, daisy-chained like SCSI devices.

Chapter 28

Docking Stations

Laptops and notebooks are very popular. The portability is a great attraction for many users, but not everyone wants to own a laptop for travel and a desktop for his or her home or office. To address this issue, manufacturers typically make available a solution that takes care of both needs.

Sharing Resources

Docking stations are an attempt to successfully merge a desktop PC with a laptop. A docking station does this by supplying the hardware that is typically not available with a laptop:

- Mouse
- External keyboard
- Larger display
- Network card for an office environment
- Local or networked printer connection

The laptop provides everything else: a CPU, a CD-ROM drive, and a floppy drive are typical. By combining the two devices, the docking station is able to function as a full desktop PC. By taking the laptop out of the docking station, you are left with only peripheral devices that cannot operate.

Some docking stations allow you to use the laptop keyboard and the video display by attaching a device to the back of the laptop that supports the other hardware (see Figure 28-1). Other docking stations require you to close the laptop and insert the laptop into a slot on the front of the station. This allows you to use an external keyboard, mouse, and possibly a larger display.

Figure 28-1. Rear-attached docking station

Same User, Different Devices

When a laptop is installed in a docking station, it has access to other devices not usually available when operating as a portable. This requires device drivers to be installed to support those docking station devices. A problem occurs when disconnecting a laptop from a docking station and booting up the device. Sometimes you can get error messages stating a particular piece of hardware cannot be found or is not functioning properly. Obviously, this is because the docking station isn't present, but ignoring the error messages isn't the best solution.

For this reason, most Windows operating systems allow you to define a hardware profile. This is a list of the hardware that should be present when the laptop is booted up. Because a hardware profile can be edited, it is a simple matter to create two hardware profiles—one for a docked laptop, one for an undocked laptop. For more information on creating hardware profiles, perform a search using the Windows Help feature; each version of Windows is slightly different in how it configures and uses hardware profiles.

Chapter 29

Basics of Networking Hardware

Networking Basics

Connecting computers together and getting them to
communicate isn't as simple as plugging in a few cables
and turning the PCs on. Some planning is involved.
The following are some items you should consider when
creating a network.

Hardware

When it comes to networking computers together, the
lowest common denominator is hardware. There are
numerous devices and cabling types to choose from; each
choice can affect things such as the speed, distance, and
cost of your network.

Chapter 30 will cover the hardware in more detail, but
a few items to know about include hubs, switches, and
routers. When it comes to wiring, be sure to read up on
Ethernet, as it is the most common type of networking
used today.

29

Protocols

PCs have to talk, and they have their own languages,
just like people. The language that PCs talk is commonly
called a protocol. But it's not that simple. A protocol isn't
just a language; it's also a collection of tools and methods
for ensuring that communication is sent, received, and
understood.

Common networking protocols in today's networks
include NetBEUI, IPX/SPX, and TCP/IP. The protocol

handles the behind-the-scenes work required to make a network function. And networks don't just use one primary protocol; many networks support multiple protocols, enabling them to communicate with other networks that don't necessarily use the same primary protocol.

Type of Network

Once all the hardware is connected and cabled together, you still need to make some choices. Just as computers can be configured in multiple ways, networks can also be configured differently. Peer-to-peer, client/server, and domain networks all exist, and it is important to know the differences between each in order to make the network function properly and efficiently. See Chapter 57 for more information on the types of networks.

Shared Resources

The power of a network is the ability to share files and resources with other users on the network. Sharing a high-speed, color printer with other users is less expensive than buying, installing, and configuring a printer on each user's individual PC. Likewise, giving coworkers the ability to access some of your files saves you from having to copy them to floppy or CD-ROM and deliver them to coworkers who then have to copy from a floppy or CD to their own PCs. The network allows files and resources to be shared and accessed as if they were on the local PC. This is one of the primary benefits of a network.

Chapter 30

Network Hardware

Networking Hardware for the PC

PCs connect using a variety of hardware. This chapter
covers the most typical component used to configure
a small to medium-size network of PCs, the network
interface card (NIC).

NICs

A network can consist of numerous hubs, switches,
routers, and other hardware, but without the PCs, the
network isn't going to get used much. Connecting PCs
is what networking was created for; the component that
allows this to occur is the NIC.

A NIC is easy to install, and most Windows operating
systems automatically configure the card for you. Some
network cards are immediately recognized by Windows
and do not even require a driver to be installed. All other
NICs, however, require that you install the driver needed
for the NIC to communicate with Windows.

Almost all new PCs use either a PCI or USB network
interface device, usually for use in an Ethernet network.

The easiest way to determine whether a network card
is installed is to look. On the back of a PC, Ethernet NICs
are fairly easy to spot. The RJ-45 jack is a little larger than
the RJ-11 jack (commonly known as a telephone jack), as
shown in Figure 30-1.

The second method for determining whether a network
card is installed is to check in the Device Manager. Open
Device Manager, and expand the Network Adapters icon
(if it exists). Any network adapters installed will be listed
here, as shown in Figure 30-2.

30

Figure 30-1. RJ-45 Ethernet NIC jack

NOTE *You should verify that any NIC you wish to install in a PC is found on the Microsoft Hardware Compatibility List (HCL). If a NIC isn't listed there, it may still work, but why take the chance?*

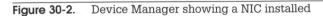

Figure 30-2. Device Manager showing a NIC installed

MAC Addresses

One additional item involved in networking and NICs is the MAC address. The Media Access Control number is a unique number assigned to every device participating in a network. The MAC address is a 48-bit binary number, but is typically represented as a six-digit hexadecimal number, such as 00-06-5B-E0-1E-26.

Because the MAC address doesn't change on a NIC, it is the number that is actually used in communicating on a network. The IP address that is assigned to a PC can change, but the MAC address is static. IP addresses are actually resolved to MAC addresses when PCs and other networking devices wish to talk to one another.

30

Chapter 31

Network Topologies

A topology is simply a way to describe how PCs and other networked devices are connected. There are two primary topologies (bus and ring) and two hybrids (star ring and star bus).

Bus

A bus topology connects all PCs and network devices via a single cable (see Figure 31-1). The advantage of a bus topology is the low cost to put it together. A disadvantage is that if the cable is cut or damaged in any way, the entire network will go down.

In a bus environment, all communication on the network is "heard" by all devices. A PC broadcasts a signal on the cable, which the other PCs receive and determine if it is directed at them; network devices ignore a signal that isn't intended for them, but they still hear the broadcast.

Ring

A ring topology connects the PCs and network devices in a ring (see Figure 31-2). Rings use a method called *token passing* to transmit data and communicate on the network. A token designates which network device (PC, router, and so forth) can "talk" at the moment. If a PC doesn't have the token, it can't communicate on the network until it gets possession.

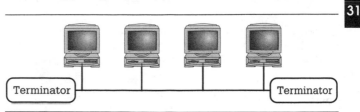

Figure 31-1. Bus topology

Rings aren't as popular as they used to be (compared to Ethernet, which uses a star topology), but they still exist. In theory, a ring can handle as many network devices as you can fit on the network. In reality, the more devices on the ring, the longer it takes for each device to obtain the token, which can increase network lag.

Star Ring

The star ring topology is a popular and widely used topology still found today (see Figure 31-3). With the popularity of Ethernet, star ring topologies have decreased in popularity, however. PCs use a special NIC to communicate with the Multistation Access Unit (MAU) that controls the token. The "star" part comes from the fact that each device is connected in a star pattern to a hub or switch that functions as a MAU. Signals on the network still flow in a circular pattern as defined by the ring topology.

Star Bus

The Ethernet standard uses a star bus topology (see Figure 31-4). All devices are connected to a central device, such as a hub or switch, and this device functions as a bus. Unlike a bus topology, if a cable is cut, the

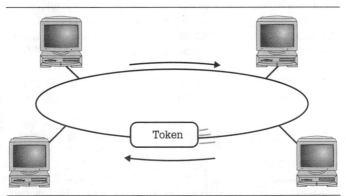

Figure 31-2. Ring topology

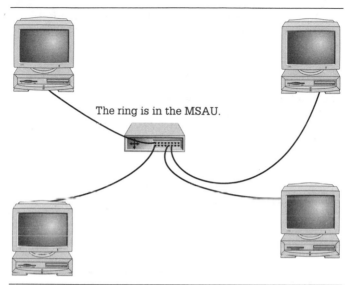

Figure 31-3. Star ring topology

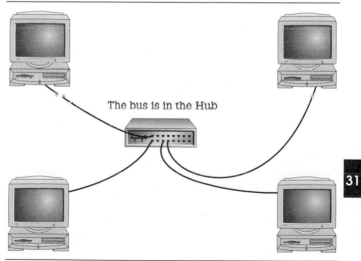

Figure 31-4. Star bus topology

other devices can still communicate on the network. Troubleshooting is also easy; if all devices connected to the bus (switch, hub, and so forth) are failing to communicate, the most likely culprit is the centralized bus device.

The star bus topology also is less susceptible to outages than a bus or ring, because each device is on its own cable connected to a central hub or switch. If one device goes down, it won't affect the other devices.

Chapter 32

Hardware Protocols

With all the different types of networking devices available, a standard for how the hardware connects becomes a necessity. The two most common methods for connecting hardware together are discussed next: Ethernet and Token Ring.

Ethernet

The Ethernet standard is the most popular method for connecting networks together. It can be set up in different forms, including 10Base5, 10Base-T, and 100Base-FX. Each variety of Ethernet describes a different way to connect devices and the hardware used.

ThickNet—10Base5

One of the earliest versions of Ethernet used a thick cable for connecting devices. This cable, also known as Thick Ethernet or ThickNet, is a special coaxial cable using the Belden 9580 standard. The coaxial cable is made up of a thick core of copper surrounded by a layer of insulation. The insulation is then covered with a braided material useful in shielding the core from electromagnetic interference. The core, insulation, and shielding is then covered by a heavy-duty cover.

ThickNet uses the bus topology, requiring each PC or network device to tap into the thick cable using a special type of hardware (called a vampire tap) that penetrates the thick cable with sharp teeth to create a connection. The vampire tap sends and receives data using this connection to the core of the coaxial cable. With a bus topology, both ends of the primary cable must be terminated using special 50-ohm terminators.

32

Maximum distance for ThickNet is set at 500 meters, and the network can theoretically run at speeds up to 10 megabits per second (10 Mbps). ThickNet is not as popular these days and has been replaced with Ethernet standards such as 10Base-T and 100Base-FX.

ThinNet—10Base2

Thin Ethernet, also known as ThinNet, is a less expensive alternative to ThickNet. The cable is thinner and easier to install. Using coaxial cable of type RG-58, ThinNet runs at speeds of 10 Mbps and can only reach lengths of 185 meters.

ThinNet uses a bus topology, but there is a limit to the number of devices that can be attached per segment: 30.

ThinNet connects to devices using BNC connectors and a T-connector (see Figure 32-1). The T-connector allows the cable to continue to run without the use of a vampire tap.

With ThickNet, both ends of the cable must be terminated, but with ThinNet, one terminator must be grounded. Adding another PC or device to the network is a simple matter of removing the terminator from the last device on the network and using another piece of cable to extend the distance to the new device. Remember to reinstall the terminator.

Figure 32-1. BNC connectors connecting to a T-connector

10Base-T

The most popular form of Ethernet today is 10Base-T (although 100Base-T is quickly closing the distance). 10Base-T defines a network that is capable of supporting speeds up to 10 Mbps using a type of cable called unshielded twisted pair (UTP). Cable distance for each segment is limited to 100 meters, but this distance can be extended using repeaters.

UTP does come in different qualities of cable, however, that allow the speed of the network to be increased beyond 10 Mbps. A category level is defined for different types of UTP. The category level defines the maximum speed supported by that level of cable. Table 32-1 defines Category 1 to 5 UTP.

Remember that 10Base-T can only run on Cat 3 or higher UTP. The cable uses an RJ-45 connector to connect to network devices. RJ-45 is similar to a phone cable, RJ-11 (see Figure 32-2).

Fast Ethernet

Although 10Base-T is the most common type of Ethernet found today, it is quickly being replaced by 100Base-T, also known as Fast Ethernet. Running at 100 Mbps, this new standard is gaining popularity both with businesses that are demanding higher speeds for their networks and with home users who want the fastest connection to the Internet possible.

Fast Ethernet is one of many new versions of the Ethernet standard that are competing to replace 10Base-T.

CAT 1	Standard phone line
CAT 2	Data speeds up to 4 Mb/s
CAT 3	Data speeds up to 16 Mb/s
CAT 4	Data speeds up to 20 Mb/s
CAT 5	Data speeds up to 100 Mb/s

Table 32-1. Standard Category Types of UTP

32

Figure 32-2. RJ-11 (left) and RJ-45 (right)

The downside is that each new version is completely incompatible with the other Ethernet varieties.

Fiber-Optic Ethernet

Fiber-optic cable uses light to transmit data at speeds in the gigabit range. But it's expensive. Fiber-optic cable can be difficult to install and is expensive to manufacture. For these reasons, fiber-optic Ethernet standards (10Base-FL and 100Base-FX) aren't quite as common. Where speed is the top requirement, fiber-optic Ethernet is the best solution.

Fiber-optic cable length limits are greater than 10Base-T or even ThickNet. Cable distances of up to 2000 meters are allowed.

Repeaters and Hubs

Before discussing the other popular hardware protocol standard, two items need to be addressed.

Repeaters can be used to extend the distances of any type of Ethernet cable previously discussed. The repeater simply takes the incoming signal (which might be weakened due to distance) and retransmits it. The advantage is that Ethernet networks can be increased in physical size and distances. For example, a collection of PCs in a 10Base-T network can only be 100 meters from the switch or hub used to connect them together. With a repeater, one or more of these PCs could be placed at a greater distance, with the repeater placed in between them and the hub/switch they would normally be required to connect to directly.

A hub is the simplest bus topology device for connecting PCs and other network devices. It contains a number of ports into which each networked device will plug using Ethernet cable. In a 10Base-T network, an eight-port 10Base-T hub allows up to eight devices to be plugged in and network-connected.

Token Ring

Token Ring is a type of topology, as discussed in Chapter 31. It functions using a token, but the physical connections resemble a bus topology. The token is passed around the ring, with each device only able to communicate when it obtains control of the token. Token Ring uses a special type of hub compatible only with Token Ring, not Ethernet.

Token Ring is not compatible with Ethernet. It also runs at different speeds: 4 Mbps and 16 Mbps. Because of these speed limitations, it is easy to see why Ethernet has replaced it as the standard hardware protocol.

Token Rings also use different types of connectors and cable. Shielded twisted pair (STP) is the commonly used cable for Token Rings and, like the categories of Ethernet cable, STP comes in its own types, listed next. But it is possible for some Token Ring environments to use UTP.

- **Type 1**   Standard STP with two pairs (most common)
- **Type 2**   Standard STP with two pairs plus voice wires
- **Type 3**   Standard STP with four pairs
- **Type 6**   Patch cable
- **Type 8**   Flat STP cable
- **Type 9**   STP with two pairs—plenum grade

32

With STP, Token Ring can support up to 260 PCs. With UTP, it can support up to 72 PCs. UTP maximum distance from the hub to a PC is 45 meters; with STP, that distance increases to 100 meters. Token Ring can also use repeaters to increase the standard maximum distances defined by the standard.

Chapter 33

Operating System Basics

The Windows operating system had some humble but important beginnings. MS-DOS (Microsoft Disk Operating System) was the predecessor of Windows 3.*x* and Windows 9*x* systems and still has a limited role in the newest operating system, Windows XP. Every technician can benefit from a working knowledge of DOS and its abilities. This chapter describes some of the most common and useful DOS concepts.

In a Nutshell

DOS is text-based. Everything is done from a command line, and, in a purely DOS system, the hardware supported is extremely limited; you won't find a GUI, and the mouse is not used. DOS will run on any processor, from the early 8086 to the latest Pentium 4 family, but no matter the hardware, DOS is still a single-tasking operating system.

Files

A file is the most basic piece of data that DOS can manage. All files consist of a filename and an extension. Filenames can be up to eight characters in length, with an extension of up to three characters.

Illegal characters for both filename and extension include the following: / \ [ ] < > + = ; , * ?.

These characters are illegal because, in some form or another, they are used with DOS commands and are therefore "reserved" characters.

Acceptable examples of DOS names include JIM.EXE and AUTOEXEC.BAT. Unacceptable examples include DECEMBER11.TXT, TWO+TWO.DOC, and FILENAME.*

DOS uses extensions to identify the application that can read or run the file. Some files have extensions that are only recognizable by the DOS operating system. For example, files with the .SYS extension cannot be opened by a word processor or spreadsheet application. They contain data in a format recognizable by DOS. Some files in DOS can be opened using the EDIT command, which can open TXT, BAT, and INI files, for example.

Files are stored and managed using drives and directories.

Drives and Directories

On bootup of your PC, DOS assigns a drive letter to each drive partition (including extended and logical) and to all floppy drives and CD-ROM drives. By default, the first floppy drive is usually assigned A:, and the primary partition (hard drive) is given C: as the drive letter. Drives can be assigned up to Z: in a DOS environment.

DOS uses a hierarchical directory structure, which organizes files into directories and subdirectories. To open a specific file, you type the command you wish to use to work on that file, then the drive's assigned letter, followed by a backslash (\) and then the directory name (followed by another backslash for each subdirectory).

For example, to open and read a file named MYTEST.TXT on the C: drive in a subdirectory called DOCS in the PERSONAL directory, you would type

EDIT C:\PERSONAL\DOCS\MYTEST.TXT

This format for specifying a file location is called the file's *path*.

Brains of DOS

Although DOS consists of numerous types of files, there are three individual files that make up the core of the operating system: IO.SYS, MSDOS.SYS, and COMMAND.COM.

If these files are not found on the primary boot drive (or are corrupt), the operating system will not load. IO.SYS allows communication between the hardware and DOS. MSDOS.SYS loads and makes up the kernel of the operating system. Without the kernel, the commands you provide to DOS cannot be executed by DOS. And finally, COMMAND.COM interprets the commands you wish to send to DOS. COMMAND.COM consists of a large but finite set of commands that are used to manipulate files. These three primary files will use other files stored in the DOS directory on the primary boot partition (for example, C:\DOS) to execute your commands.

Chapter 34

DOS User Interface

Unlike a Graphical User Interface (GUI), DOS provides the user with a simple but easy-to-use interface for getting work done: the command prompt. From the command prompt, a variety of simplified instructions can be issued. This chapter presents some of the basic commands for moving around in DOS.

The Prompt

The DOS prompt, or command prompt, is the flashing cursor you are presented with when booting up into DOS (see Figure 34-1).

The prompt, by default, is set to show you the directory in which you are currently working. Typically, a user sees c:\> when they are at the root of the C: drive. The flashing cursor is waiting for a command to be typed in.

Where Am I, and What's Here?

Look at the command prompt and you'll know immediately what directory you're using. As an example, if you see C:\DOS\, you know you're currently set to do work in the DOS directory on the C: drive. To find out what files are in the DOS directory, you have to issue a command that

Figure 34-1. The DOS prompt

will give you that information. Type DIR at the command prompt to get a complete listing of the files, file sizes, and the modified timestamp, as shown in the example in Figure 34-2. Subdirectories will be given a <DIR> to designate their status.

DIR is used to give you a listing of a directory's contents. If the directory includes a lot of files, the list will quickly scroll up the screen, and you will not be able to read all the contents. To prevent this, DOS includes command controls, called *switches,* that add functionality to DOS commands. For example, two switches for the DIR command are /w and /p. By typing DIR /w, you will be provided with a condensed file listing, minus some of the details. Typing DIR /p presents the information a page at a time. To continue to the next page, hit the SPACEBAR.

You'll notice that filenames are shown in the 8.3 notation, meaning 8 characters for the filename and 3 characters for the extension. Even the new operating systems, like Windows 2000 and XP, still use the 8.3 notation when running a DOS window. For longer filenames, these operating systems use a tilde (~) to replace the eighth character and indicate that the name is longer than can be displayed.

```
C:\>DIR
Volume in Drive C is
Volume Serial Number is 1734-3234
Directory of C:\

DOS                 <DIR>                09-03-96    9:34a
COMMAND     COM               34222      04-01-94    4:33p
AUTOEXEC    BAT               14         04-03-00    11:55a
WINDOWS             <DIR>                11-07-99    1:34a
CONFIG      SYS               34         04-03-00    4:36p
MIKE                <DIR>                09-03-99    8:15a
JUNK        DOC               55677      05-13-99    10:03a
COMMAND     COM               23222      09-03-96    4:33p
9 file(s)  72233 bytes
            18288834 bytes free
```

Figure 34-2.   Example of DIR at the root of the C: drive

Moving Around

You've seen that files are stored in directories and subdirectories. To access the directories, DOS provides a command that allows you to move around within the directory structure. The CD command (Change Directory) allows you to specify the directory you wish to view. To access a subdirectory of the current directory you are in, simply type CD and the name of the subdirectory. Alternately, if you know the complete subdirectory path, you can also type that and go directly to deeper subdirectories. Both of the following commands are valid from the C. prompt:

- **C:>\ CD DOS**   Changes the DOS prompt view to C:>\DOS\

- **C:>\ CD \PERSONAL\DOCS**   Changes the prompt view to C:>\PERSONAL\DOCS\

If you type in an incorrect directory name or incorrect subdirectory path, you will receive a message indicating DOS cannot find the specified path. At that point, you can use the DIR command to view the directories (remember that <DIR> indicates a directory) and then change to directories individually until you move down through the directory structure.

Changing Drives

To move between drives, the DOS command is the simplest yet. At the prompt, just type the drive letter followed by a colon and hit the ENTER key. To change from the C: drive to the floppy drive, you type **C:>\ A:**, press ENTER, and then type **A:>** (now you're working on the floppy drive).

If you are working in a subdirectory (such as C:>\DOS\) and change to another drive letter, when you change back to the original drive (D:, for example), you will find yourself back in the same subdirectory you were in when you left—C:\DOS.

Making and Removing Directories

Another easy DOS command is MD (Make Directory). Type MD, a space, and then the name of a directory you wish to create. In the following example, typing MD GAMES creates a directory called GAMES in the directory in which you are currently located:

1. Make a new directory by typing the following at the C:>\PERSONAL\ prompt: MD GAMES (then press ENTER)

2. Next change to that directory by typing the following at the C:>\PERSONAL\ prompt: CD GAMES (this issues a CD command to change to the new directory)

3. Finally, you'll see that you are working in the correct directory, C:>\PERSONAL\GAMES\

To delete a directory, you use the RD (Remove Directory) command. The directory *must* be empty, however, to delete it. Use the DEL command to delete individual files. The following example shows how to remove the GAMES directory created earlier:

1. At the C:\PERSONAL\GAMES\ prompt, type the following: CD \PERSONAL (then press ENTER)

2. At the C:\PERSONAL\ prompt, type the following: RD GAMES (then press ENTER)

3. You can issue a DIR command on the C:\PERSONAL\ directory to see that the GAMES subdirectory has been removed

Chapter 35

Files

Because DOS is all about files and directories, there are a few items that are specific to working with them.

Attributes

All files in DOS possess characteristics called attributes. These attributes define four values that affect how a file is used or seen by the operating system and installed applications:

- **Hidden**   Hidden files do not show up in the list when you issue a DIR command from the DOS prompt.

- **Read-Only**   Read-Only files cannot be modified or deleted using standard DOS commands.

- **System**   System files are special files used by the operating system; the attribute lets you do a search using wildcards that can distinguish between system files and non-system files.

- **Archive**   The Archive attribute is used by applications that perform backup operations. This attribute is turned on or off by the backup program, informing the program whether a file has recently been backed up.

To see the attributes for a file, simply type ATTRIB followed by the path and filename. You can also use wildcards to see the attributes for a certain selection of files. When using the DIR command, letters representing the attributes are written to the left of each file: A for Archive, H for Hidden, S for System, and R for Read-Only. You might see something similar to this:

A H   C:\AUTOEXEC.BAT

A SHR C:\IO.SYS

In the case of the IO.SYS file, it has the Archive, System, Hidden, and Read-Only attributes all turned on. Attributes may be enabled or disabled. To enable an attribute, use + and the letter of the attribute *after* the ATTRIB command and the filename. Typing C:\>ATTRIB IO.SYS –H would disable the hidden attribute and allow IO.SYS to be visible when issuing a DIR command.

Wildcards

If you have many files in a directory, chances are that some of the files start with the same letter. Some files may even have the same filename, except for a few characters. DOS provides you with the ability to perform standard commands on multiple files using wildcards. Wildcard examples include * and ?. The * symbol represents multiple characters, and ? represents one character. As an example, if you want to see all files in a directory that end with the extension .TXT, you could type DIR *.TXT. All files ending with .TXT would be shown. Using ? is slightly different, in that it can take the place of one character; typing DIR jan2?.TXT would show you all files starting with jan2 and ending with TXT: Jan21.TXT, Jan22.TXT, Jan28.TXT would be visible, but not Jan30.TXT. You can use wildcards for almost all DOS commands, including DIR, DEL, COPY, and MOVE.

Copying and Moving Data

Copying a file does not remove the original file from its current location, but moving a file will. To perform either task, type COPY or MOVE and then the filename followed by the destination path. The destination path is where the file will be copied or moved. You do not necessarily have to be working in the directory that contains the file you are attempting to copy or move; if you know the current location, you can specify the path and the filename together. For example, typing COPY C:\AUTOEXEC.BAT E:\TEMP\ copies the AUTOEXEC.BAT file to the TEMP directory on the E: drive. Wildcards work with the COPY and MOVE commands also, so you can manipulate multiple files with one command. Typing COPY C:\TEMP*.TXT E:\TEMP\ copies all files ending with .TXT into the TEMP directory on the E: drive.

35

Xcopying

A variation of the COPY command, XCOPY allows you to copy files and directories in one quick step. There are many switches that allow you to control what is copied and to where, so type XCOPY ? at the DOS prompt to get a complete listing and descriptions of the switches that can be used.

Chapter 36

DOS Hardware Configuration

Hardware has to talk to the operating system in order to function properly. DOS has special files that allow this communication to take place. CONFIG.SYS contains information on device drivers, and AUTOEXEC.BAT helps programs access hardware devices.

CONFIG.SYS

Device drivers are used by devices that want to talk to the operating system. These drivers are usually created by the hardware manufacturers and are provided on CD or floppy disk. When you install the hardware and the driver, the CONFIG.SYS file is updated to reference these driver files (usually ending in the .SYS extension).

The CONFIG.SYS file loads the device drivers into memory on bootup.

AUTOEXEC.BAT and TSRs

On bootup, certain programs are installed automatically. These programs are called TSRs (Terminate and Stay Resident) and work well with DOS. TSRs are executed by typing the name of the TSR at a DOS prompt. They reside in memory and stay active until the computer is shut down. TSRs load common programs that are used constantly, like MOUSE.COM, which gives control of a mouse to the operating system. The AUTOEXEC.BAT file loads the TSRs. On bootup, the commands contained in the AUTOEXEC.BAT file execute. Each line of the file contains code that either loads a TSR or sets a system configuration parameter. This file is normally found on the root of the C: drive.

With GUI-based operating systems (such as Windows 95 or Me), the CONFIG.SYS and AUTOEXEC.BAT files can be bypassed by pressing F8 on bootup and choosing to boot to a DOS prompt. You can also choose a selection that will allow you to load each file line-by-line, which can help you to troubleshoot faulty drivers and TSRs.

Tools for Working with Drives

When working with hardware in a DOS environment, there are a few basic tools that you should be aware of and know how to use. They include the following:

- **SYS**   Typing the SYS command at a prompt copies the three primary DOS files to the partition you specify. You use this, typically, to make a bootable floppy disk.

- **FDISK**   This tool allows you to view and manipulate drive partitions, including primary, extended, and logical partitions.

- **FORMAT**   To prepare a drive for file storage, it must be formatted. This is what creates a FAT or NTFS file system. Be careful with this command, as it is not something you can undo.

- **EDIT**   A quick text-editing tool that allows you to open and view BAT, TXT, and INI files that are common in a DOS environment or DOS-based operating system.

- **SCANDISK**   This utility will scan a drive you specify for damaged clusters, bad sectors, and overall problems.

Chapter 37

DOS Memory Management

Even though the Windows operating systems generally
do a good job of managing your PC's memory, on a DOS
system, you need to understand how memory is controlled
and how it works.

Memory Basics

DOS can only handle a 1 megabyte (1MB) memory address
range. This memory is broken into two separate areas:
conventional memory and reserved memory. Conventional
memory is RAM set aside for programs. Reserved memory
is used by other system RAM and ROM chips that the CPU
will access. Conventional memory is 640K, and the address
range is 00000h to 9FFFFh. Reserved memory is 384K, and
the addresses are from A0000h to FFFFFh.

Reserved Memory

Reserved memory is available to ROM and RAM chips
that also need to use system memory. The addresses
they use are already defined by their manufacturers and
usually cannot be changed. Hardware such as the system
BIOS and video card use reserved memory addressing so
that DOS has a consistent location to reference when
using these devices. Figure 37-1 shows how memory is
divided between reserved and conventional memory.

Memory Management Goal

Memory is limited, so the goal of memory management is
to reduce the amount of conventional memory that is in
use. A large part of reserved memory is typically unused.

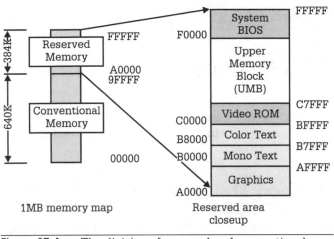

Figure 37-1. The division of reserved and conventional memory

This area is called the Upper Memory Block (UMB) and contains addresses C7FFh to F0000h. By having programs use UMB memory, conventional memory is freed up.

To use the UMB, you must edit the CONFIG.SYS file by adding the following line after the DEVICE=C:\DOS\HIMEM.SYS line:

    DEVICE=C:\DOS\EMM386.EXE

EMM386.EXE allows the UMB to hold device drivers and programs. To actually install a driver or program into that memory space, you must first tell DOS that you will use UMB. You do this by adding the following line to CONFIG.SYS:

    DOS=UMB

Next, to load a driver or program into UMB, change its line in the CONFIG.SYS file by changing DEVICE= to DEVICEHIGH=. Loading a TSR into UMB is done the same way in the AUTOEXEC.BAT file, but it uses LOADHIGH or LH in front of the TSR to be loaded.

Extended Memory

The early days of DOS allowed only the first 1MB of memory to be used for loading TSRs and programs into memory. Later, a technique was developed that allowed more memory to be accessed using an extra wire on the address bus. This modification only freed up about 64KB of memory, but it was enough to allow a few extra memory addresses that could be used in addition to the conventional memory. This new memory range, starting at address FFFFFh, is called extended memory.

Extended memory is not used directly by DOS; modification of the CONFIG.SYS file is necessary (similar to the changes made for the UMB) for programs to use it. Add the line DEVICE=C:\DOS\HIMEM.SYS to your CONFIG.SYS file, as described in the previous section. Next, you'll specify that the memory is accessible by DOS by adding the line DOS=HIGH.

Programs can then be loaded by DOS into extended memory. This is handled automatically by DOS.

Chapter 38

Viruses

Understanding the different types of viruses that can harm a computer system will help you to identify any infections and prevent your system from being corrupted or damaged by a virus.

Boot Sector

The Master Boot Record (MBR) on the hard drive can be infected by a specific type of virus called a *boot sector virus*. This type of virus can corrupt, delete, or modify the MBR. Boot sector viruses remain in memory and attempt to replicate themselves using floppy and Zip disks that can accidentally or intentionally be booted. This causes the infected disk to place a copy of the boot sector virus on the new PC.

Executable

This type of virus imbeds itself in an application, either commercially or custom-written. Many times these files masquerade as games or small screensavers that can be distributed using e-mail. Sent as attachments, once the executables are run, the virus infects the system and performs whatever actions it has been programmed to execute.

Macro

Macro viruses are written using special programming features built into commercial applications. Most macros are not bad, but since the applications are not able to distinguish between a useful macro and a malicious macro, this type of virus has become more common than boot sector and executable viruses.

Trojan Horses

Trojan Horses (also called Trojans) are not really viruses. They are small applications that perform both actions that are visible to the user and actions that occur behind the scenes and are not visible to the user. These hidden actions can be either damaging or simply annoying. Popular versions of a Trojan include spy programs (called *spyware*) that are installed without the user's knowledge. These programs then monitor user activities and attempt to relay the information to other parties.

Fighting Back

One of the easiest ways to prevent viruses and Trojans is to install an antivirus program. These antivirus programs use lists to scan the computer systems for known viruses. These lists (called virus signature files) should be updated regularly (daily, weekly, monthly) and allow you to scan your system for the latest viruses found on the Internet. They work by comparing known viruses and the patterns of code they contain against files on your system. Questionable files are then brought to your attention along with choices such as deleting the file, cleaning the file, or quarantining the file.

Damage from Trojans and spyware is usually prevented by running programs that search out these types of applications. They work in a similar fashion to antivirus programs; they maintain a list that contains known Trojans and spyware programs, and scan your system for items on the list. Any items found can be removed.

It is important that Trojan and virus scanners be updated regularly. It is even more important that they be run regularly. Try to use scanners that allow you to automate the process so that it can be done without you having to remember to do it; the best scanners allow you to automate not only the scanning but also the downloading of the latest signature files to maintain a list of the most current culprits.

Chapter 39

Hard Drives

Hard Drives

Windows 9x supports a variety of hard drive sizes, speeds, and interface types. Once a hard drive has been installed in a Windows 9x PC, it must be configured to properly store data.

39

FDISK

A common tool used to configure hard drives with Windows 9x is FDISK. FDISK is a DOS-based tool that can be run from a hard drive or a boot floppy disk. With a new hard drive installation, the functions of FDISK are typically performed by the Windows 9x CD installation. The following steps are performed:

1. The hard drive is partitioned.

2. The drive is formatted and the file system is created.

3. Sectors and clusters are determined based on the partition size and the file system used.

Partitioning

Partitioning a Windows 9x hard drive is done using FDISK. Insert a boot floppy disk for Windows 9x and boot up the PC. At the command prompt, type **FDISK** to get to the FDISK menu, shown in Figure 39-1.

From this menu, you can create a primary partition, set an active partition, delete a partition, and display current partition information. Depending on your selection from this menu, you will also be able to create extended partitions and logical partitions.

```
                    Microsoft Windows 98
                   Fixed Disk Setup Program
          (C)Copyright Microsoft Corp.  1983 - 1998

                        FDISK Options

Current fixed disk drive: 1

Choose one of the following:

1. Create DOS partition or Logical DOS Drive
2. Set active partition
3. Delete partition or Logical DOS Drive
4. Display partition information


Enter choice: [1]


Press Esc to exit FDISK
```

Figure 39-1.   FDISK menu

File System Types

The file system used in Windows 9x PCs will determine
how much data can be stored on each cluster. Remember
that when data is written to a disk, the data is stored in
sectors, with each sector holding a specific number of
clusters. The maximum size of the partition you create
determines the sector/cluster size, which in turn affects
the efficiency of the data storage on the hard drive.
Windows 9x uses either the FAT or FAT32 file system.

FAT

FAT (or File Allocation Table) can be used on hard drive
partitions of up to no more than 2GB of storage space.
FAT is also sometimes seen as FAT16. Table 39-1 provides
the number of sectors/clusters by partition size.

Remember to create partition sizes to minimize the
amount of wasted space. This typically means using a
partition size of less than 1023.9 MB.

FAT32

FAT32 supports partitions of up to 2 terabytes of storage
space. FAT32 was introduced with Windows 95 OSR2.

If the DISK Makes a Partition This Big	You'll Get This Many Sectors/Clusters
16 to 127.9 MB	4 sectors/clusters
128 to 255.9 MB	8 sectors/clusters
256 to 511.9 MB	16 sectors/clusters
512 to 1,023.9 MB	32 sectors/clusters
1,024 to 2,048 MB	64 sectors/clusters

Table 39-1. Partition and Sector/Cluster Sizes for FAT/FAT16

FAT32 is a more efficient file storage system, but is not fully compatible with pre-Windows 95 OSR2 systems.

39

Note in the table that partitions of over 32,767 MB require 64 sectors/clusters, making it the most inefficient partition size. With today's larger hard drives (100 GB or more), a substantial amount of space is used inefficiently when creating a single partition; it is recommended that larger hard drives be partitioned with more than one extended and/or logical partition.

Long Filenames vs. Short Filenames

Because Windows 9x systems are DOS systems at the core, there is still an issue with filename length. DOS and Windows 3.x used a naming standard referred to as 8.3. This meant the filename could be no longer than eight standard characters (letters and numerals) and was saved with a three-character extension. For compatibility with older systems, Windows 9x systems still support the 8.3 standard, but also support filenames up to 255 characters. Remember, when saving or moving files from Windows 9x to older DOS-based systems, two files, DataBackupJan2003.xls and

If FDISK Makes a Partition This Big	You'll Get This Many Sectors/Clusters
512 to 8,191 MB	8 sectors/clusters
8,192 to 16,383 MB	16 sectors/clusters
16,384 to 32,767 MB	32 sectors/clusters
32,768+ MB	64 sectors/clsuters

Table 39-2. Partition and Sector/Cluster Sizes for FAT32

b2003.xls, need to be renamed to an nvention in order to be usable.

Formatting the Hard Drive

After creating the partition on a Windows 9*x* hard drive, the file system (FAT or FAT32) will be set for the hard drive. The only way to change the sector/cluster size at this point is to delete a partition and re-create it with a different partition size. At this point, the partition will be formatted before an operating system or data can be written to it.

To format a hard drive, from a command prompt, type **format** *drive letter* and press ENTER. As an example, if you have created a primary partition (C:) and an extended partition (D:) and wish to format C:, you would type **format c:**, as shown in Figure 39-2.

Windows 9*x* will only install on a partitioned and formatted hard drive. For this reason, Windows 9*x* systems use a Setup disk (with the FDISK and format commands on it). Once the hard drive is partitioned and formatted, installation of Windows 9*x* from floppy disk or CD-ROM (the preferred method) can begin.

```
A:\>format C:/s

WARNING:  ALL DATA ON NON-REMOVABLE DISK
DRIVE C:  WILL BE LOST!
Proceed with Format  (Y/N)?y


Formatting  30709.65M
Format complete.
System transferred

Volume label (11 characters, ENTER for none)?

32,197,017,600 bytes total disk space
        262,144 bytes used by system
32,196,755,456 bytes available on disk

        491,520 bytes in each allocation unit.
        982,455 allocation units available on disk.


Volume Serial Number is 3166-11D9
```

Figure 39-2.   Formatting a partition

Chapter 40

Installation

Installing Windows 9x

Installation of 9x is a fairly simple process if you follow the correct procedures. Windows 9x includes Plug and Play (PnP) functionality, which has reduced the amount of work involved in identifying and setting up the hardware in the PC. Before beginning any installation, first determine that the PC will meet the Windows 9x minimum requirements.

Minimum Requirements

Windows 9x has very few minimum requirements, but ignoring any one of them can cause the installation to abort or result in a PC that does not function correctly.

For Windows 9x installation, the following requirements exist:

1. 486DX/66 MHz CPU with 24MB of RAM
2. 400MB of hard drive space minimum
3. Video adapter capable of supporting no less than 640×480 resolution with 16 colors
4. Keyboard
5. Mouse, CD-ROM, and sound card are also recommended

Check Microsoft's Hardware Compatibility List at www.microsoft.com/hcl/ for an up-to-date listing of all hardware determined by Microsoft to be supported by the Windows version you are installing. The list includes items such as motherboard, sound cards, video cards, mouse, CD-ROM drives, and other hardware. You can also check a manufacturer's web site for drivers or updates regarding hardware and Windows 9*x* compatibility.

Installation consists of two parts:

1. DOS-level install
2. Graphical install

DOS-Level Install

With a new installation of Windows 9*x*, the installation process begins either with the insertion of the Setup disk or by placing the Windows 9*x* CD in the CD-ROM drive. Some PCs allow you to begin the Windows installation by booting from the CD, but not all. Windows 98 CD-ROMs and later are bootable, but Windows 95 and earlier require the Setup disk (see Figure 40-1).

During the DOS-level install, the hardware will be scanned and checked for compatibility. Drivers will be installed to allow for the basic graphical installation process to start. One or more reboots will occur.

Figure 40-1.   Windows 95 Setup disk

Problems

Most Windows 9*x* installations complete without
any problems. In the instance in which the installation
does not complete or does not function properly, some
troubleshooting options are available:

- Most hardware incompatibility errors show up during
  the DOS-level install. The error messages received
  usually give you an idea as to what piece of hardware
  is not "playing well" with the others. Check the HCL ·
  and the manufacturer's web site to make sure the
  hardware is 100 percent compatible with the version
  of Windows you are installing.

- During the Graphical install, any problems detected
  can usually be skipped over (such as ignoring the
  request for hardware drivers by clicking the Cancel or
  Skip button), but not always. Windows 9*x* installations
  provide errors messages that can be checked on the
  Microsoft Knowledge Base. Log files are also stored at
  the root of the C: drive (check for SETUPLOG.TXT,
  DETLOG.TXT, and BOOTLOG.TXT) and can be viewed
  at a command prompt by typing **edit** *filename* or **type**
  filename │ **more**. Examining the logs can sometimes
  help in determining why an installation is not
  completing or is giving errors.

Graphical Install

After the DOS-level install steps have been completed,
the Graphical install (also called the GUI install) will begin.
Before the major installation begins, however, you need
to select the type of installation—for example, Typical for
a standard installation, or Portable for a laptop/notebook
installation (see Figure 40-2) and provide a valid Product
Key (see Figure 40-3). You must enter this key before any
files will be copied from the CD to the hard drive.

You are then asked where to install Windows 9*x* (the default
is C:\Windows, but you can choose a different location).

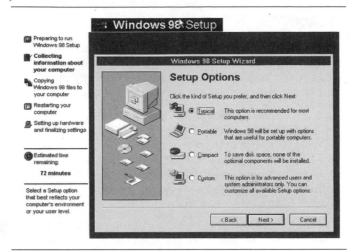

Figure 40-2. Setup options

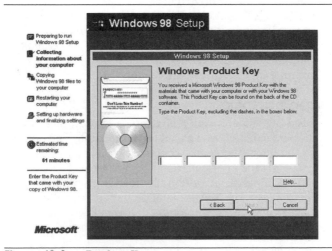

Figure 40-3. Product Key

Next, the majority of the Windows 9*x* files will begin to be copied from CD to the directory location you selected

After successfully installing the operating system, the next step involves installing the software and drivers for any Plug and Play hardware installed in the PC. Windows 9*x* installations do a good job of finding most (or all) of your hardware, but in some instances you will be prompted to supply a floppy disk or CD-ROM with the necessary files to complete the hardware installation. Once these files are supplied (and possibly after a few reboots), the Windows 9*x* desktop will be loaded and Windows is ready to go.

Upgrading

If an existing operating system is to be upgraded, check the HCL to ensure that the hardware will function properly with the new operating system. It is also important to verify that the software currently installed on the system will be compatible with the new operating system. After upgrading, it is not uncommon to find that older applications will not work with the new OS. Backing up your data before the upgrade is also recommended.

In the instance of an upgrade, the only difference between an upgrade procedure and a "clean" install is that the upgrade procedure will begin at the Graphical Install portion of the installation.

40

Chapter 41

Troubleshooting

Troubleshooting Windows 9x Installations

Windows 9x operating systems come with numerous GUI tools and command-line tools to assist with troubleshooting common Windows installation problems. There are also error messages that can be used to narrow the search for a problem piece of hardware or software. Your main goal is to get the Windows 9x desktop up and running; at that point, the installation process is complete. There are, however, some issues that can stop the installation process.

DOS-Level Errors

There are a few errors that can pop up during the DOS-level install. Table 41-1 lists some of the more common error messages and possible fixes.

Error Message	Possible Fix
No Boot Device Present when booting off the startup disk	It is possible the startup disk is defective or damaged. Also make sure that the PC BIOS is set to boot off a floppy disk before the hard drive or CD-ROM drive.
Windows has Detected that Drive C: does not contain a valid FAT partition	Double-check that a primary partition exists and that it is set to be the active partition.

Table 41-1. DOS-Level Errors and Possible Solutions

Error Message	Possible Fix
Windows Setup requires *XXX* amount of available drive space	If the hard drive isn't formatted, try to format the drive first. If the drive is formatted, make sure that the minimum required hard drive space for installing Windows exists before running Windows Setup.
MSCDEX error "No CD-ROM detected"	In Windows 9*x* setups, this usually indicates a lack of CD-ROM, a misconfigured CD-ROM drive, or a CD-ROM drive that is not compatible with the HCL. Also check the CONFIG.SYS and AUTOEXEC.BAT files for the correct CD-ROM settings. Refer to the hardware documentation for the correct settings.
Not Ready Error on CD-ROM	Some new CD-ROM drives are fast—sometimes too fast for the DOS-level installation to catch up. Press the R key to retry the installation. The Windows installation CD may be damaged.

Table 41-1. DOS-Level Errors and Possible Solutions
(continued)

Graphical Installation Errors

Table 41-2 shows graphical installation errors.

Error	Possible Solution
Can't read CAB files	Check CD-ROM for damage (scratches or cracks). It is also possible to run the installation by copying the CAB files to the hard drive. Copy all files located in the Win9*x* directory on the CD into a hard drive directory you have created. Run Setup from that directory.

Table 41-2. Graphical Installation Errors and Possible Solutions

Error	Possible Solution
This system already has an OS	This is a common message seen when upgrading an earlier version of Windows 9x to a more recent version (Windows 95 to 98, for example). If you are using a full install CD instead of an upgrade CD, perform the following steps to force the installation to continue: 1. Exit Setup. 2. Type **c:** at the command prompt. 3. Type **cd \system** and press ENTER. 4. Type **ren setupx.dll setupx.re1** and press ENTER. 5. Type **ren setupx.w95 setupx.re2** and press ENTER. 6. Run Setup.

Table 41-2.   Graphical Installation Errors and Possible Solutions (continued)

41

Other Installation Errors

One of the more common installation problems after Windows has installed is a system lockup. This can occur for a variety of reasons, but the most common involves hardware that is not compatible with the operating system you have installed.

- If you are unable to boot up to a normal Windows screen, attempt to first boot up in Safe Mode. Do this by pressing F8 before the normal Windows start screen pops up. To be safe, just tap the F8 key every five to ten seconds after booting the PC. When you get a list of options on the screen, select Safe Mode and press ENTER. If you can boot into Safe Mode, it's a good possibility that the Normal startup installation is being stopped or slowed down by a piece of incompatible hardware (either the physical hardware or the software driver).

- Check the Windows logs (stored on the root of the boot drive), specifically the DETLOG.TXT file, which sometimes lists devices that are impeding bootup.

- BOOTLOG.TXT can also help by giving you a line-by-line description of the bootup process. If you know where in the bootup the system is crashing, boot into Safe Mode as in Step 1, but instead of choosing Safe Mode, select Step by Step Confirmation to give a Y or N answer on loading specific files and drivers. When you see the file from BOOTLOG.TXT that is causing problems, choose N to skip loading it. If Windows boots normally after this, remove the hardware in question until it can be determined why the hardware is causing lockup.

If the PC can successfully load the desktop (Start button and desktop icons, including System Tray icons), you have successfully installed Windows 9x.

Chapter 42

Windows 9x Bootup Process

Now that you have a basic understanding of the DOS operating system, you'll find that the Windows 9x bootup process has many DOS features built-in, running behind the scenes.

The Important Files

There are three files that Windows 9x systems use in order to boot properly: IO.SYS, MSDOS.SYS, and COMMAND.COM. Without these three files, the Windows operating system (specifically, the GUI) will not load and function properly.

Also, Windows 9x systems can use the AUTOEXEC.BAT and CONFIG.SYS files, but with the addition of the Registry, Microsoft began an attempt with Windows 9x to move away from storing application and system data in standard files like SYSTEM.INI and WIN.INI. However, these files still serve a function. Below is a discussion of the bootup process for Windows 9x.

Bootup

When you first turn on a Windows 9x machine, the BIOS performs its standard bootup functions, checking hardware and assigning IRQs. At a particular point in the bootup process, a file called IO.SYS is loaded. This file has been discussed elsewhere in this book, but one of its functions is to check to see if F8 has been pressed.

Pressing the F8 key while Windows boots up will cause a Windows Startup menu to appear. From this menu, you

42

can choose a Normal bootup, a Safe Mode bootup, and other options. Safe Mode is useful for technicians because it allows them to troubleshoot a Windows operating system using basic drivers for the hardware found. No fancy drivers are installed and a slimmed-down version of Windows is loaded.

If F8 is not pressed, Windows 9x systems will move into the Graphical User Interface (GUI) loading phase.

WIN.INI and SYSTEM.INI

During the GUI loading phase, the WIN.INI and SYSTEM.INI files are also loaded. The Registry holds the majority of system and application data, but these two files are still used occasionally by Windows 9x.

WIN.INI can be edited to make changes to the look and feel of Windows 9x systems. This file holds settings that affect screensavers, fonts, and other display features. It can also be configured to load certain programs automatically on bootup.

The SYSTEM.INI file is slightly different. It contains information from the initial bootup and the hardware and software settings found during the Power On Self Test (POST).

Windows 9x systems still use SYSTEM.INI regularly. One important reason for its continued use is backwards compatibility with Windows 3.x applications. Many of the Windows 3.x applications would keep their settings in the SYSTEM.INI file.

Windows Desktop

As Windows 9x systems load up, the familiar desktop will appear. During this process, the system will appear to be "ready to go," but many users know that even once the desktop appears, it can still be a minute or longer before

Windows is ready to use. The reason for this delay is the "behind the scenes" configurations that are occurring.

The Registry contains a lot of information; not only does it hold settings about Windows, but it also contains settings about the hardware in your PC, the software installed, and much more. When the Windows desktop is loading, a lot of information is being pulled from the Registry to configure exactly how the Windows 9x system will appear, what programs will be ready to use, and what hardware will be displayed.

Another function being performed is the loading and execution of the Startup applications. These programs can include such items as antivirus applications and power and video settings. Most of the startup applications appear on a Windows 9x system in the lower right corner, also known as the System Tray.

Once all the hardware and software has been recognized and been made available to Windows, the desktop is ready to use.

42

Chapter 43

System Files

Standard Windows 9x System Files

Windows 9x operating systems are based on DOS. Therefore, it is no surprise that many of the behind-the-scenes files that Windows uses are holdovers from the DOS and command prompt days. A working knowledge of these files is necessary to support Windows 9x systems.

IO.SYS

IO.SYS is the first of three important Windows 9x system files. When first booting Windows 9x systems, you can access a Startup menu that gives you more options than just the standard Windows bootup to the desktop. It is the IO.SYS file that checks for the keyboard's F8 key to be pressed (see Figure 43-1). If this file becomes damaged or corrupted, Windows 9x may not boot. Booting from an emergency boot disk can get around this problem, as well as allow you to overwrite the damaged IO.SYS file.

```
Microsoft Windows 98 Startup Menu
=================================

  1. Normal
  2. Logged (\BOOTLOG.TXT)
  3. Safe mode
  4. Step-by-step confirmation
  5. Command prompt only
  6. Safe mode command prompt only

Enter a choice: 1




F5=Safe mode  Shift+F5=Command prompt  Shift+F8=Step-by-Step confirmation [N]
```

Figure 43-1. Use the F8 key to call up the Startup menu.

WIN.INI

WIN.INI is a holdover from the earlier versions of Windows, specifically Windows 3.*x*. Although Windows 9*x* and later systems no longer need to use the WIN.INI file (thanks to the Registry), it is still useful for checking out bootup settings. To access it, click Start, then Run, and type **WIN.INI** before clicking the OK button. You can also run SYSEDIT from the Run window to see WIN.INI and other Windows system files (such as AUTOEXEC.BAT).

SYSTEM.INI

SYSTEM.INI is another holdover from the earlier versions of Windows, mainly because it takes over the roll of CONFIG.SYS from Windows 3.*x* systems. Windows 9*x* and later systems still need to use the SYSTEM.INI file to allow for backward compatibility with older software. Even if you are not running any older Windows 3.*x* software, SYSTEM.INI is still checked for at bootup, and a damaged or missing SYSTEM.INI file will give you an error message on boot. Use an emergency boot disk to boot up to Windows and repair it.

The Registry

The Registry is the one place where all software and hardware settings are stored. Prior to Windows 9*x* operating systems, the Registry did not exist and software and hardware configurations were kept in separate files (usually INI files). This caused confusion and a lot of problems when programs and hardware would use the same filenames; overwriting or deleting INI files was a common problem.

A basic knowledge of the Registry and its components is useful in troubleshooting and supporting Windows 9*x*. The following are the components that make up the Registry and a brief description:

- **HKEY_CLASSES_ROOT (HKCR)**   Stores basic class objects used in Windows 9*x* systems. These class objects usually refer to system functions.

- **HKEY_USERS (HKU)** Stores information on the user accounts that exist on the Windows 9*x* system (such as wallpaper, file storage settings, and screen size).

- **HKEY_CURRENT_USER (HKCU)** Stores information on the currently logged-in user. When multiple users log in to Windows 9*x* systems, HKCU mirrors the information stored in HKU for that logged-in user.

- **HKEY_LOCAL_MACHINE (HKLM)** Contains nonuser-related data and configuration settings for the PC. Device drivers and settings are an example.

- **HKEY_CURRENT_CONFIG (HKCC)** A copy of HKLM, but can sometimes contain different data depending on the user who is logged in. For example, one user might have the CD-ROM disabled when they log in. This information overrides the HKLM information when this user is logged in.

- **HKEY_DYN_DATA (HKDD)** RAM memory can store some system information, allowing the PC to operate faster. The data that can be used is stored in HKDD and loaded into RAM memory when the PC is booted up.

43

REGEDIT

Windows 9*x* systems come with a very powerful tool to edit the Registry. REGEDIT, shown in Figure 43-2, is a useful tool for performing manual changes or updates to Windows settings. But REGEDIT can also cause Windows 9*x* systems to crash or even fail to boot if an improper setting is added or changed in the Registry. Take care when working with REGEDIT.

To access REGEDIT, click Start, select Run, type **REGEDIT**, and click OK.

Before performing any changes to the Registry, be sure to back up the current Registry settings. To perform this task, click Start, select Run, type **SCANREG/BACKUP**, and click OK.

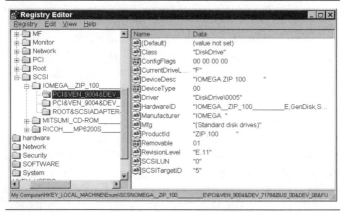

Figure 43-2. REGEDIT tool with Windows 9x

You can also back up the files that make up the Registry (SYSTEM.DAT and USER.DAT) by copying these two files (they might be hidden, so be sure your View Options allow you to see all files, including hidden files) to a safe folder on your hard drive (C:\REGBACKUP, for example).

To restore the Registry, you can either click Start, select Run, type **SCANREG/RESTORE**, and click OK, or, after booting from a boot disk, copy SYSTEM.DAT and USER.DAT from your backup location to C:\WINDOWS\SYSTEM.

Chapter 44

Optimizing and Maintaining

Service Packs, Hotfixes, Patches, and Windows Update

Windows 9x operating systems, like all software, require periodic maintenance. Microsoft provides each operating system with patches and fixes for problems that are reported or noted during use. Microsoft also releases enhancements to the operating system through regular updates.

Service Packs

Service packs are software bundles that attempt to fix a number of bugs found in Windows. Service packs are typically cumulative, meaning that Service Pack 2 will contain the fixes found in Service Pack 1 along with additional problem resolutions. Service packs can be downloaded from Microsoft's web site or can be obtained on CD-ROM.

Although Microsoft uses the term "service pack," there have been variations over the years to the term. Microsoft has also released "Security Service Packs" and "Customer Service Packs." The thing to remember is that if the words "service" and "pack" are used, it is probably best to install it. These are fixes that Microsoft has decided are important for the function and security of the Windows operating system.

For a complete listing of service packs, go to www.microsoft.com and do a search for **service packs**. The current page includes service packs for the newest operating system, Windows XP, and links to previous service packs for older operating systems.

Hotfixes/Patches

Frequently, Microsoft will encounter a problem with Windows that is reported by a small percentage of the Windows user community. In this instance, Microsoft sometimes chooses to create a "quick fix" in the form of a software patch. This patch (also called "hotfix") is typically released to fix one or two specific problems. These problems can be related to Plug and Play drivers, hardware components, or other circumstances not reported by a large portion of Windows users.

Hotfixes can also be downloaded from the Microsoft web site. When in doubt, always read the documentation with a hotfix to determine if the patch should really be installed in your OS. Many times, a hotfix has no effect on a user's system because the Windows operating system in question does not exhibit the symptoms described in the documentation.

When Microsoft releases service packs, frequently it bundles some or all of the hotfixes into the service pack. This does not mean that the service pack contains *only* hotfixes. Service packs should always be installed, and frequently contain fixes or updates for which no specific hotfix exists.

Windows Update

Starting with Windows 98, Microsoft includes a built-in feature to its operating systems—Windows Update (see Figure 44-1). Windows Update can be run from the Start menu and from within Internet Explorer. Windows Update accesses the Microsoft web site to provide the reader with a one-stop-shop for all Windows 9*x* updates, specific to their OS.

When running Windows Update, the system prompts you to install some software updates on the system. You can answer YES or NO, but if you answer NO, the Windows Update will not be able to function properly. You can still access the site to determine what updates and patches are available.

If you answer YES to installing the software updates, Windows Update runs a scan of your OS and provides a detailed list of available updates. These updates fall into different categories: security, recommended, and miscellaneous.

- **Security updates**   Should always be installed if possible.

- **Recommended updates**   Should be read in detail to determine if the Windows 9x system can use the update.

- **Miscellaneous updates**   Items that might make Windows look different or provide some enhancement (European currency conversion, for example). Installing these updates is typically low risk.

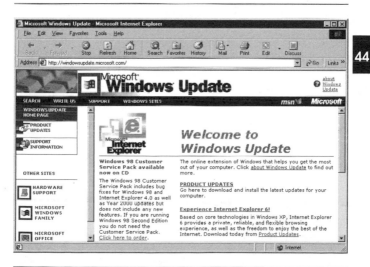

Figure 44-1.   Windows Update

Chapter 45

Troubleshooting

Troubleshooting Windows 9*x*

No operating system is perfect, and Windows 9*x* systems require their fair share of troubleshooting.

Windows 9*x* systems crash, lock up, and exhibit all types of behavior that defy explanation. Given this advanced knowledge, you need to remember to do one thing—back up the system.

"Backing up" Windows 9*x* systems can mean different things:

- Backing up personal files.
- Backing up everything.

Backing Up Personal Files

Backing up personal files can be done using numerous tools. Windows 9*x* systems come with a tool called Backup. Found in Start | Program Files | Accessories | System Tools, this program allows you to back up files to Zip disks, other hard drives, CD-RW devices, or even one big file. In the case of corrupted or lost data, restoring your personal files simply means running the Backup program again and pointing to the location of the last backup.

45

NOTE *Personal files should be backed up regularly, clearly labeled, and time-stamped in some fashion. Nothing is more confusing than having to restore files and also having to figure out which CD or Zip disk contains the most recent backup.*

Backing Up Everything

Another option is to backup everything. This includes personal files, the Windows operating system, and all of your applications. Although Windows 9x doesn't provide this ability as a standard tool, various third-party products do allow you to create images of your hard drives. Like a photo, these products take a "snapshot" of your drive at a specific point in time. This snapshot is converted into a compressed file and written (usually) to a CD-R disc or a network drive.

NOTE *Never store system images on the actual hard drive being backed up. Some products allow you to do this, but it isn't recommended because the backup is intended to be used if the hard disk becomes corrupted or needs a complete restore.*

Reboots

Windows 9x locks up. The first symptom can be the lack of mouse response or a blue screen that suddenly appears with system failure information on the screen. Typically, rebooting is the only recourse. If a reboot doesn't fix the problem, and the problem persists or can be duplicated, you need to examine log files and error messages to determine whether a hardware or software conflict is causing the lockup. Ask most techies, though, and they'll tell you that 90 percent of Windows 9x problems can be fixed by rebooting. Rebooting clears the memory and reloads the Registry, frequently "fixing" small quirks and bugs in the system.

VxD Problems

A common problem with Windows 9x systems involves device drivers. Frequently, Windows 9x will crash or hang on bootup with an error message telling you that "filename.VxD could not load." Typically, you can choose to ignore this by pressing any key to skip over it, but the problem will pop up again on the next bootup. You can usually fix this by searching for the filename referenced in the error message and removing it from either the SYSTEM.INI or WIN.INI file.

Shutdown Problems

Windows 98 and Me both have known issues with shutting down. Shutdown issues can usually be resolved by visiting the PC manufacturer's web site and downloading a shutdown patch for Win98/Me. Microsoft also has numerous fixes for this problem in its Knowledge Base. Read each article carefully, as some of the fixes should only be applied to specific models or in certain specific circumstances.

45

Chapter 46

Windows NT Structure and System Files

Windows NT (versions 3.5, 3.51, and 4.0) looks very similar to the earlier Windows operating systems; the differences are in the underlying structure. However, NT was designed to be a more robust operating system than the earlier versions. With that in mind, the developers redesigned the entire way the system worked.

NT Components

The Windows NT operating system is composed of three key parts (see Figure 46-1):

- Hardware
- NT Executive
- Subsystems

New File System

With the introduction of NT, Microsoft also introduced a new file system, replacing the old FAT/FAT32 with a

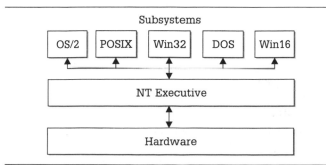

Figure 46-1. Windows NT core components

more reliable and full-featured file system. NTFS allows for larger hard drives and larger partitions, and includes some features that FAT did not support:

- Larger partitions of up to 2 terabytes
- Long filenames of up to 255 characters
- MFT (Master File Table) to allow for a backup of the file table
- Backward compatibility with FAT/FAT32
- Transaction logging to document for accidental failures, reboots, and lockups
- Granular file and folder security

Bootup

NT boots up a little differently than Windows 9x systems, too. The GUI is very similar once the desktop is up and running, but getting there uses a different path.

The boot partition contains the files that make up the Windows NT operating system. The system partition contains the specific files used to boot Windows NT.

Windows NT also supported dual-boot systems, allowing for Windows 9x systems to run on PCs running Windows NT.

Security

Security with Windows NT boils down to three categories:

- Accounts
- Groups
- Permissions

Accounts

Access to NT files or applications cannot occur until the user authenticates with a valid username and password.

With Windows 9*x*, the user can cancel the logon operation, but Windows NT systems require a logon. Therefore, each authorized user must have an account. The most powerful account on a Windows NT system is the administrator account.

Groups

User accounts with Windows NT can be collected into groups. Groups are useful for granting similar permissions (or denials) to files, folders, and applications. Windows NT provides administrators with powerful tools that are unavailable with Windows 9*x* systems. These tools allow for better access control to a network and its resources.

Permissions

Every file, folder, application, and command that Windows NT can use has the ability to be controlled. This control is handled by using permissions. Permissions define what a user account or group can and cannot do. With the introduction of Windows NT, standard permissions were introduced:

- Full Control
- Modify
- Read & Execute
- List Folder Contents
- Read
- Write
- System Partition Boot files

46

Required Files

Windows NT has four files required for bootup:

- **NTLDR**   Reads the BOOT.INI file on bootup to find the boot partition
- **BOOT.INI**   Contains the location on the hard drive of the boot partition and each OS installed

- **NTDETECT.COM** With NT, detects hardware on bootup and loads drivers
- **NTBOOTDD.SYS** Loads drivers for SCSI drives, if applicable (only for SCSI controllers without ROM BIOS)

Chapter 47

Disk Management

Windows NT Disk Management

Windows NT can use standard DOS/Windows 9x–based
tools for managing local hard drives. But Windows NT
also comes with a powerful, new tool for managing
your drives.

Disk Administrator

Windows NT uses a graphical tool called Windows NT
Disk Administrator to manage hard drives. You can
perform partitioning and formatting from this tool, as
well as set up some of the RAID options that came
standard with Windows NT.

Disk Defragmentation

NT did not come with a native disk defragmentation tool.
A third-party product must be purchased and installed to
perform this function.

ScanDisk

Right-clicking a drive in Windows NT and select Properties.
Choosing the Tools tab (see Figure 47-1) gives you the
option to perform basic disk scans on the drives. Click
the Check Now button to start the scan.

47

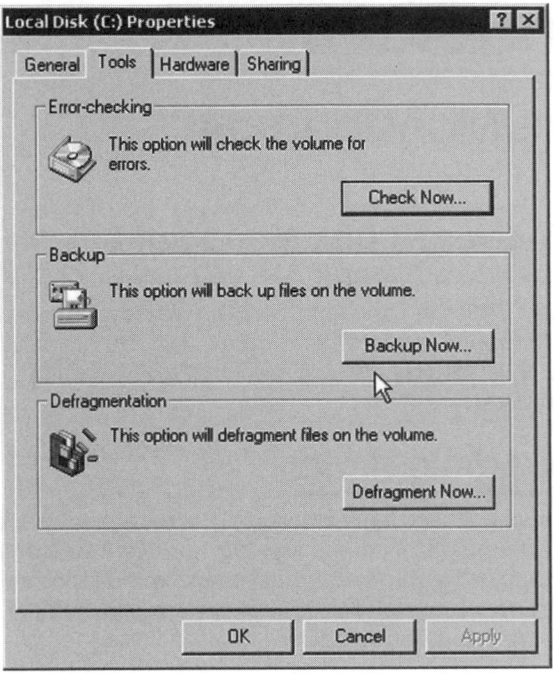

Figure 47-1. Tools menu and the Check Now button

Chapter 48

Troubleshooting and Upgrading

Besides the Microsoft Knowledge Base (located at www.microsoft.com), Microsoft has provided built-in tools for troubleshooting common Windows NT issues. Two options are available for troubleshooting common Windows NT bootup problems.

Emergency Disk Repair

Windows NT allows the user to create a special bootup disk (similar to a Windows 9x startup disk) that contains the important files necessary to boot up a failed Windows NT machine. This special disk is called the Emergency Repair Disk (ERD) and is stored on a single floppy disk. Using this disk, you may be able to successfully boot a failed Windows NT machine and attempt to repair the operating system from within the Windows NT GUI.

To create the ERD, you run the RDISK command from a command prompt. Follow the instructions onscreen to create it. After it is created, label the disk with "Emergency Repair Disk for *Machine Name* and *Date*." Be sure to store the disk in an accessible but secure location.

Startup Options

Windows NT does not have the same range of bootup options, such as Safe Mode, that Windows 9x systems possess. On bootup, the user is given two choices: normal bootup (default) and VGA mode bootup. A timer counts down to 0, and when 0 is reached, the normal bootup will occur if the user does nothing or selects normal bootup.

One other option exists in case of problems. After you accept the default or choose the bootup mode described in the previous paragraph, you will see the text "Press Spacebar NOW to invoke Hardware Profile/Last Know Good menu." Pressing L after the SPACEBAR will load the previous settings. Pressing L tells Windows NT to attempt to load the bootup settings that were in effect prior to the last bad bootup (if one exists). Pressing the SPACEBAR, if no problems exist, simply loads the same bootup options as the last time the Windows NT machine was booted.

Upgrading Windows NT

Upgrades to Windows NT exist in the form of hotfixes and service packs. Hotfixes generally attempt to repair one or two known problems with Windows NT and are released frequently by Microsoft. Service packs, which are released less often, typically include patches to numerous problems as well as upgrades to files and tools in Windows NT. The last service pack released for Windows NT was Service Pack 6. Service packs are cumulative, meaning installing one service pack will install the repairs from previous service packs.

Chapter 49

Installation

Windows 2000 is actually sold in four versions: Professional, Server, Advanced Server, and Data Center Server. The A+ Exam covers the installation of Windows 2000 Professional.

Minimum Hardware Requirements

Windows 2000 Professional requires a minimal level of hardware for a successful installation to complete. Table 49-1 shows the Microsoft minimum recommendations.

NOTE *Keep in mind that Microsoft's recommended requirements are typically not acceptable for real-world usage. Speed and efficiency are likely to be reduced by adhering to the minimum requirements. Table 49-2 has more realistic recommendations for the hardware.*

Component	Minimum Requirement
CPU	Intel Pentium 133 MHz
Memory	64MB
Hard disk	2GB w/650MB of free space
Network	None
Display	Video adaptor and monitor with VGA resolution
CD-ROM	12X (not required if installing over a network)

Table 49-1. Minimum Microsoft recommendations

49

Component	Minimum Requirement
CPU	Intel Pentium II 350 MHz
Memory	128MB
Hard disk	6.4GB w/2GB of free space
Network	Modern PCI network card
Display	Video adaptor and monitor with SVGA resolution, capable of High Color (16-bit) display
CD-ROM	24X (not required if installing over a network)
Floppy Disk Drive	High-density

Table 49-2. More Realistic Hardware Requirements for Windows 2000

And finally, remember to verify all hardware with Microsoft's Hardware Compatibility List (HCL), found on the Microsoft web site at www.microsoft.com/hcl.

Decisions, Decisions

Whether you are doing a completely new installation of Windows 2000 Professional or an upgrade, you have to make a few choices during the installation:

- **Partition** Windows 2000 Professional, by default, attempts to install itself on the active partition. This usually is C:\WINNT, but if you are performing an upgrade, the directory may be different. You can also choose a different location for the boot partition (where the operating system files are stored).

- **Networking options** Windows 2000 Professional is designed to operate in a networked environment. Therefore, certain key components are installed by default, including TCP/IP, Client for Microsoft Networks, and File and Printer Sharing. Additional network options can be selected during the installation.

- **Language and locale** Select the correct language and time zone during the installation.

- **File system**   Windows 2000 Professional supports
  FAT16, FAT32, and NTFS. You can convert a
  FAT16/32 file system to NTFS after the installation
  is complete or during the actual install.

Options: Upgrading to
Windows 2000 Professional

Here are some important items to remember when
performing an upgrade to Windows 2000 Professional:

- You can upgrade from Windows 9*x* systems and
  Windows NT Workstation (3.51 and 4).

- Boot from the Windows 2000 Professional CD
  when upgrading from NT 4.

- When upgrading from a Windows 9*x* system, some
  applications may need to be reinstalled.

- Install any service packs that exist for Windows 2000
  Professional after the upgrade.

- Windows 2000 does not support VxDs files that
  enabled applications in Windows 9*x* to access
  hardware directly. This is not supported by the
  NT operating system.

- Windows 2000 Professional does not support
  third-party compression.

Chapter 50

Boot Sequence

Windows 2000 Professional Boot Sequence

Windows 2000 Professional requires that the following files be located in the root directory of the system partition:

- NTLDR
- BOOT.INI
- NTDETECT.COM
- NTBOOTDD.SYS (only for SCSI controllers without ROM BIOS)

Advanced Options

An Advanced Options menu is available (similar to Windows 9x systems) by pressing the F8 key at boot. The following options are available:

- **Safe Mode**   Opens Windows 2000 Professional in a limited mode consisting of basic drivers for the keyboard, mouse, video, and hard drive(s).

- **Safe Mode with Networking**   Safe Mode with additional files loaded to support network connectivity.

- **Safe Mode with Command Prompt**   Loads basic drivers but presents the user with a standard DOS-style command window.

- **Enable Boot Logging**   Saves boot information to a file called NTBTLOG.TXT.

- **Enable VGA Mode**   Boots Windows 2000 Professional normally (not in Safe Mode), but loaded with VGA

50

drivers to support basic video. This is useful for
troubleshooting the installation of video cards.

- **Last Known Good Configuration**   Windows 2000
  Professional makes a backup of the Registry on every
  successful startup. LKGC allows the system to attempt
  to restore itself to an earlier boot, which is useful in
  the case of a bad hardware or software installation
  that crashes the normal boot.

- **Debugging Mode**   Sends information to a COM port.
  Connecting a laptop or other PC to the Windows 2000
  Professional PC via a serial cable allows an
  administrator to perform remote maintenance and
  testing via the COM port.

Dual Booting

Windows 2000 Professional supports dual booting with
Windows 9x systems. The partition must be FAT16 or
FAT32. Windows 9x must be installed first. Installing
Windows 2000 Professional will prompt the user, asking
if a dual-boot system is desired.

Chapter 51

Windows 2000 Drive and File Maintenance

Windows 2000 has new functionality in the standard file maintenance tools that wasn't present in earlier versions of Windows. For the majority of file-related maintenance tasks, the tool of choice is Disk Management (see Figure 51-1). Disk Management is an MMC snap-in (see Chapter 52 for more information on MMC).

FDISK

One of the biggest changes in terms of drive management and configuration is the abandonment of FDISK. Windows 2000 now allows for configuration of hard drives through

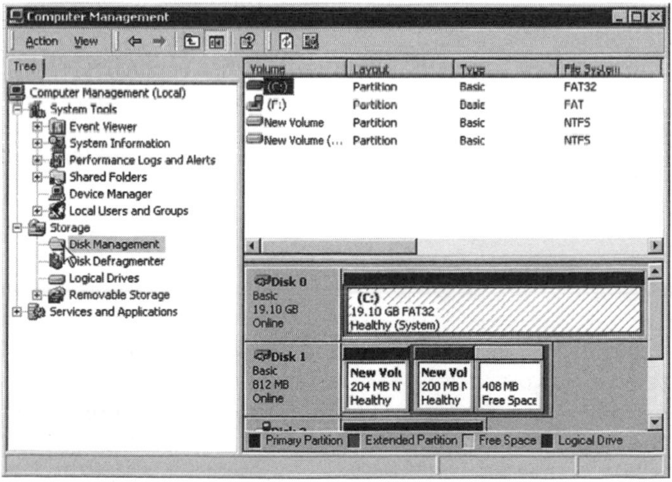

Figure 51-1. Disk Management in Windows 2000

Disk Management. The functions of the GUI are a welcome
change from the old-style FDISK command-line screen.

Basic vs. Dynamic Disks

With the introduction of Windows 2000, hard drives now
fall into two classifications:

- **Basic disks**   Regular hard drives with standard
  partition tables

- **Dynamic disks**   Hard drives that do not use partition
  tables, but allow for some new configurations

Dynamic disks are more useful in a Windows 2000 Server
machine than in a Windows 2000 Professional desktop.
The following features are included for dynamic disks in
Windows 2000 Professional and Server:

- **Spanned volume**   A volume comprising multiple
  drives

- **Striped volumes**   Two or more drives with data
  split over the drives by using alternating writes

Windows 2000 Server also includes these features with
dynamic disks:

- **Mirrored drives**   Two or more drives that share
  identical data

- **RAID 5 drives**   Three or more drives that use parity
  to compensate for a failed drive

Partitioning a Basic Disk

Using Disk Management, partitioning a basic disk is as
simple as right-clicking the drive and choosing to create a
partition. Selections include the ability to make a primary
or extended partition. Extended partitions allow you to
create logical partitions as well. Right-clicking a partition
also allows you to make it the active partition, which is
where Windows 2000 will look for the boot files.

Upgrading to a Dynamic Disk

To change a basic disk to a dynamic disk, right-click an existing basic disk and select Upgrade to dynamic disk. Verify your choice, and the disk will be upgraded. The description of the disk will change from Basic to Dynamic.

NOTE *Reverting back to a basic disk will result in loss of all data. Back up all data before choosing Revert to Basic Disk.*

Create a Dynamic Volume on a Dynamic Disk

To create a dynamic volume on a dynamic disk, right-click a dynamic disk and choose Create Volume. Which options you are provided depends on how many dynamic disks are present on your system.

Chapter 52

Windows 2000 Microsoft Management Console (MMC)

Windows 2000 incorporates a new tool into the operating system that replaces many of the Windows NT management tools. This one tool, the Microsoft Management Console (MMC), allows you to manage Windows 2000 Professional without having to switch back and forth between separate tools.

MMC Shell

The MMC by itself is an empty shell (see Figure 52-1). It becomes useful by installing *snap-ins*, small management

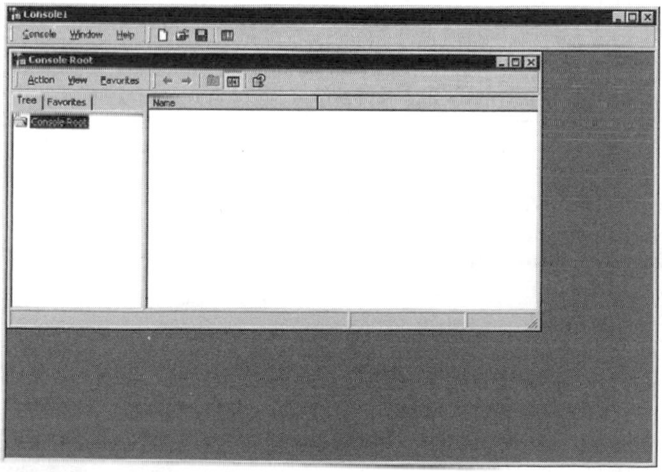

Figure 52-1. The MMC shell

tools that are provided by Microsoft and third-party developers. The snap-ins can be installed individually, but you may also install multiple snap-ins into the same shell, allowing you to access many management tools from within one window.

To open the MMC shell, select Start | Run, type **MMC**, and then press ENTER.

Snap-ins

With a blank MMC shell, you can install snap-ins by performing the following steps:

1. Select File | Add/Remove Snap-in.

2. Click the Add button.

3. From the Available Snap-in window, choose the tool that you wish to use.

4. Click Add (you can also continue to select more tools to add until you're done).

5. Click Close.

6. Click OK when you're finished, and you'll see that your MMC shell has some new additions.

Using the Snap-ins

Using snap-ins is as easy as clicking each tool. If the tool has more features, click the + symbol to the left of the tool name (see Figure 52-2) to see more details and functions of the snap-in.

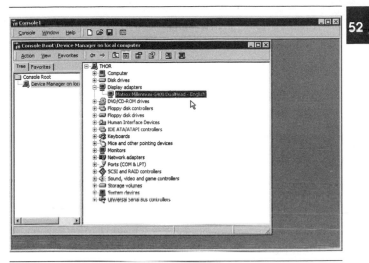

Figure 52-2.   Device Manager as a snap-in

Chapter 53

Windows 2000 Control Panel

The Windows 2000 Control Panel didn't change much
from Windows 9x. The few changes are highlighted here.

Add/Remove Hardware

When adding or removing hardware in Windows 2000,
there have been a few changes to the procedures involved
compared to the procedures used in Windows 9x. You
can still use the Add/Remove Hardware Wizard for legacy
devices. The wizard is accessed from within the System
Properties. Either right-click My Computer and choose
Properties, or open the System applet from within the
Control Panel. Change to the Hardware tab, and click the
Hardware Wizard button. Plug and Play devices will
automatically be detected, but you can still choose to select
the hardware manually. Have all device drivers (on floppy
disk or stored on the hard disk) handy, as Windows 2000
will detect most, but not all, new hardware.

Add/Remove Programs

What would a revised Add/Remove Hardware Wizard be
without a matching Add/Remove Programs Wizard? Using
the wizard, you can install and remove third-party software,
as well as uninstall and reinstall Windows components.
One nice new feature is the ability to see the size of
programs that are currently installed, as well as the Last
Used On date. This date helps to determine whether
a program is used frequently or rarely.

TIP *If a program is rarely used, click the Remove button to free up some space!*

Notice there is no Startup Disk option. With Windows 2000, the emergency repair process has changed. See Chapter 50 on troubleshooting Windows 2000 bootup problems for more information.

Administrative Tools

There's a new tool in the Windows 2000 Control Panel called Administrative Tools. As the name suggests, you will find a collection of GUI tools here to manage your Windows 2000 PC.

System Applet

Opening the System applet in Control Panel will display some new options with Windows 2000. You will see five tabs:

- **General**   Displays general information about your PC, including the operating system version, service pack level, RAM, and registration information.

- **Network Identification**   This tab displays the information relating to how your PC is connected to a network. Options to join a workgroup or domain are available.

- **Hardware**   As mentioned earlier, you can run the Hardware Wizard from this screen, as well as troubleshoot hardware installation problems (see Figure 53-1). Driver signing information is given here, and you can access the old Device Manager by clicking the corresponding button.

- **User Profiles**   Multiple users may use this Windows 2000 PC, so you can manage the accounts here.

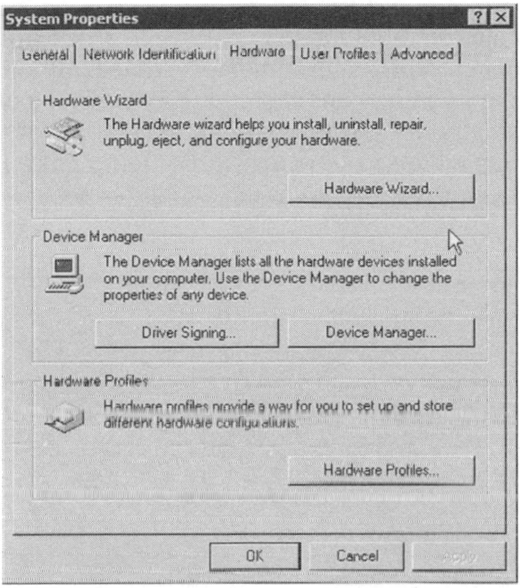

Figure 53-1.   The Hardware tab of the System applet

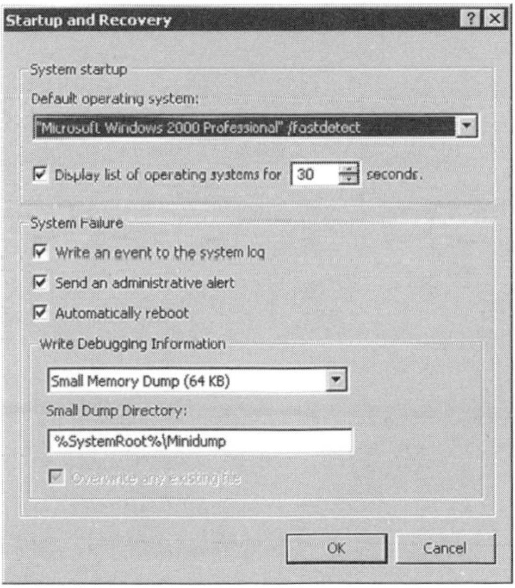

Figure 53-2.   Performance settings can be modified from the Advanced tab.

- **Advanced**   You can set performance options here, which affect how memory and drive space are used. You can modify environment variables (although seldom needing user attention anymore), as well as define startup and recovery options (see Figure 53-2), such as where to save a memory dump if the PC crashes or whether to automatically reboot.

Chapter 54

Maintaining Windows 2000

Once you have Windows 2000 Professional installed, your job isn't over. Normal day-to-day activities are required to keep Windows running efficiently.

Routine Maintenance

A couple of items are now available to help you keep your Windows drives healthy. Right-click any hard drive and choose Properties. Click the Tools menu and click the Check Now button to examine the disks for any physical problems (see Figure 54-1). After running Check Disk, click the Defragment Now button to analyze your disk.

Figure 54-1 Use this tool to Defragment or Check your hard disks.

Windows will provide a recommendation as to whether your drive should be defragmented.

TIP *Perform a defragmentation regularly to keep drive access speeds efficient.*

Hotfixes, Service Packs, and Windows Update

Although these items have been covered in other chapters, it is important to remember that Windows 2000 will function better in the long run if you pay attention to keeping the system files patched and updated. A hotfix should be installed if the problem it repairs is determined to be present on your Windows 2000 system. A service pack should be installed as soon as it is available, as it will contain security and bug fixes that affect all Windows 2000 systems. And finally, pay attention to Windows Update (see Figure 54-2) found on the Start menu. Visit it frequently to keep your system up-to-date with the latest fixes released by Microsoft.

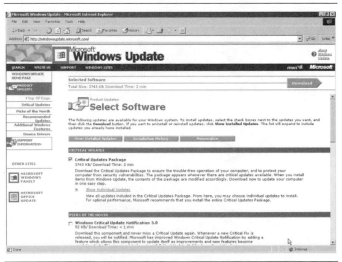

Figure 54-2. Windows Update and Windows 2000

Backups

You may have noticed an extra button on the disk Properties page in Figure 54-1. The Backup Now button allows you to back up your important files. Clicking it opens the Backup tool, shown in Figure 54-3.

This tool enables you to back up files to a hard drive, Zip disk, tape, or other removable media. The wizard will walk you through the correct steps. Click the Backup Wizard button to begin the process.

Restoring files is done from the same tool. Click the Restore Wizard button, and the wizard will step you through the process of restoring any damaged or deleted files.

There is also a Schedule Jobs tab, which allows you to automate your backup if you decide you want to perform a backup operation on a continuing basis.

Recovery Console

You will use a new tool called Recovery Console to attempt to repair a failed Windows 2000 PC. In Windows 9x

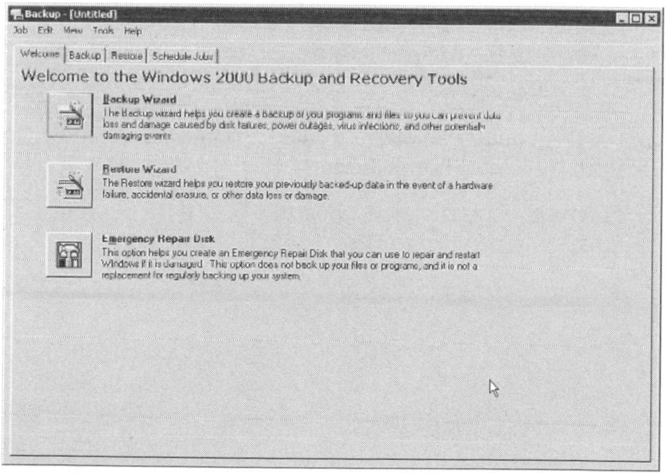

Figure 54-3.   Backup tool

systems, this is comparable to the Safe Mode/Command Prompt Only option.

To start the Recovery Console, boot your PC from the Windows 2000 CD-ROM. If it attempts to Autorun, reply No. Change to a command prompt (type **CMD** in the Start | Run dialog box) and change to the CD-ROM drive letter. Next, type **\i386\winnt32 /cmdcons**. Follow the directions to install the Recovery Console tool. When finished, you will see a Recovery Console option every time the system boots up.

The Recovery Console looks like a DOS-style screen and has many of the same commands, such as DIR, CD, and FORMAT. Using this tool, you can restore the Registry (using an ERD; see the next section), rebuild partitions, and overwrite corrupted system files from the CD.

Optional: ERD and Boot Disks

In Figure 54-3, there is another button called Emergency Repair Disk. Click this button to create a disk that contains basic partition information and bootup files. This disk is *not* bootable, but can be used with the Recovery Console to assist with recovering a failed Windows 2000 system.

Creating boot disks for Windows 2000 requires four floppy disks. Perform the following steps on a Windows 2000 PC to create the boot disks:

1. On the Windows 2000 CD-ROM, run MAKEBT32.EXE from the \BOOTDISK folder.

2. Follow the instructions onscreen to create the four disks, and be sure to label them as directed.

Chapter 55

Windows XP Control Panel

Windows XP has two views of the Control Panel: Classic View and Category View.

Classic View

Windows XP can display the Control Panel in a format that is similar to previous editions of Windows. With the Classic View, the applets (icons) represent Windows tools used to make changes to Windows XP settings. Familiar applets such as Mouse, Fonts, and Add Hardware continue to function in the same way.

There are some new icons even in the Classic View. Applets such as Game Controllers, Speech, and Scanners and Cameras add new controls to the Windows operating system for some technologies that are becoming more popular.

To switch from Classic View to Category View, click the text Switch to Category View on the left-side panel.

Category View

Category View is an attempt by Microsoft to simplify the large (and growing) number of applets that Control Panel contains. By grouping similar applets by category, Microsoft has attempted to help the user quickly find the correct tool.

Categories include:

- Appearance and Themes
- Network and Internet Connections

- Add or Remove Programs
- Sounds, Speech, and Audio Devices
- Performance and Maintenance
- Printers and Other Hardware
- User Accounts
- Date, Time, Language, and Regional Options
- Accessibility Options

To switch from Category View to Classic View, click the text Switch to Classic View on the left-side panel.

Chapter 56

Windows Network Protocols

The Windows operating systems are capable of communicating over a network using many different network protocols. This chapter includes descriptions of the four most popular protocols used by Windows operating systems. With the exception of NetBEUI, the other protocols are all routable; this means that they not only are useful in a LAN environment, where all PCs and networked devices are on the same subnet, but can also be used in a WAN environment.

IPX/SPX

Although IPX/SPX is slowly being phased out of Microsoft operating systems, this protocol, designed by Novell for its NetWare operating system, is still found in modern networking environments. The protocol has a reputation for being fast and efficient when it comes to memory.

NetBEUI

Created by IBM, NetBIOS Extended User Interface (NetBEUI) became the default protocol for early versions of Windows. NetBEUI is a small protocol but very fast; the files that it needs installed for Windows to use it are few, compared to other protocols. Its primary drawback is that it is not routable, making it useful only for small LANs with no outside communication (Internet or WAN) with other networks (via a router or other gateway). Windows 2000 and Windows XP no longer provide NetBEUI as a built-in protocol; it can, however, still be installed from the CD-ROM.

AppleTalk

AppleTalk was designed by Apple Corporation and is a
fully routable network protocol. It is similar to IPX/SPX
in speed and size. Windows operating systems support
AppleTalk to allow for communication with older Apple
computers on a network. Apple now provides support for
TCP/IP, so AppleTalk is really only useful for older Apple
computers.

TCP/IP

Called the "Protocol of the Internet," Transmission
Control Protocol/Internet Protocol (TCP/IP) is, in actuality,
a collection of networking protocols. UNIX operating
systems were the first to use TCP/IP, a protocol originally
designed by the U.S. Department of Defense.

Windows 98/Me/2000/NT/XP use TCP/IP as the default
protocol. Windows 95 will support TCP/IP, but it is
installed separately, not by default. TCP consumes large
amounts of memory and isn't as fast as AppleTalk or
IPX/SPX. Where TCP/IP shines is in its reliability. The
Internet uses TCP/IP because it is universally supported,
reliable, and well documented. See Chapter 59 for more
information on the Windows default networking protocol.

Chapter 57

Network Operating Systems

In an environment where communication between PCs, printers, servers, scanners, and other devices is a necessity, the PCs must support a network operating system. This is simply an operating system with built-in support for the protocols and services a network uses.

In a networked environment, resources can be shared between users; files can be stored in a central location (server) or on a particular PC, with users having access to files and services. All types of printers, including ink jet, dot matrix, and color printers, can be made available over the network to users, reducing hardware costs involved in putting a printer on every user's desk. There are other benefits to working in a networked environment; some benefits depend on the type of network that is implemented. This chapter describes three standard types of networks that are compatible with Windows operating systems.

57

Peer-to-Peer

The most basic type of network involves each user's PC being available to other users on the network. In this type of network, servers can also coexist, but peer-to-peer networks evolved because the cost of servers was simply too high for small to midsize networks to justify. There was a need for users to be able to share files and resources using the hardware at hand and with simple setup.

Peer-to-peer means just that—a user PC talks to a user PC. Servers in this type of network are simply a more powerful peer than a desktop PC. In actuality, all PCs on the network act in a type of server role. The person sitting in front of the PC at the moment becomes the administrator for that PC's files and resources.

The following are known limits or weaknesses with peer-to-peer networks:

- **Lack of security**   Each PC has its own security rules; therefore, anyone needing access to a PC's resources must have a user account created on that PC. In a large network, this becomes a nightmare for administrators, who need to keep track of usernames, passwords, and shared resources to which they may or may not have access.

- **Backups**   With data residing on multiple PCs, it becomes difficult to back up all the data. Simply organizing a backup strategy and a schedule can become a full-time job.

- **No logon required**   With Windows 9x systems (which are typically used in a peer-to-peer network), it is a simple matter to click Cancel on the logon screen and bypass a normal logon. Peer-to-peer network security is simple to disable.

There are some strengths to peer-to-peer, however. Costs can be reduced since peer-to-peer networks typically consist of desktop PCs and shared resources such as printers, Zip drives, and CD-ROM drives. Peer-to-peer is also fairly easy to configure. Compared to other types of networks, peer-to-peer has one of the shortest learning curves in order to maintain it, which can mean a reduced IT staff.

Client/Server

The client/server network is similar to the peer-to-peer network, but for a few changes:

- Requires all users to log on to their PC with a password

- Requires all users to store files on a dedicated PC (called a file server)

- Increases the power of the file server(s) by adding larger hard drives, faster processors, and more RAM

With these simple changes, you have upgraded what was a peer-to-peer network to a client/server network with added security. The users cannot gain access to the file servers if they do not have a valid logon name and password. The user still has access to his/her own PC, but access to any files or resources managed by the servers will be denied without proper authorization. This turns a normal PC into a client. The server will "serve" clients who have provided a valid username and password.

Backing up data is also simplified. All critical files should be stored on the file server. Backing up the local data stored on the server hard drives can be done quickly using automated software for the task.

Windows 9x systems are not designed to act as servers. Microsoft released Windows operating systems especially designed for this task. Windows NT 4 Server and Windows 2000 Server are the two most popular Microsoft server products to run in a client/server environment. Novell supports its NetWare products as a competitive server product.

57

Domains

In a Microsoft domain configuration, we build on the client/server environment and change a few things:

- Increase security by requiring all users to log on to a special server, called a logon server

- Define each user's access permissions at the server level

Domains are a Microsoft creation, but they mimic many earlier NetWare functions. In a nutshell, domains are Microsoft's way of grouping resources, servers, PCs, and other devices for ease of management. All devices in a domain can be configured in a very controlled way. Administrator accounts on the servers have permission to define what user accounts can do, what files they can access, what printers they can use, and even what time of day they can log on! As you can see, moving to a domain environment adds a lot of control to a network that peer-to-peer and client/server environments do not possess.

There are drawbacks, however. Domains require the existence of Windows NT 4 Server or Windows 2000/2003 Server. These are more costly operating systems than the Windows 9x family. The management of domain networks also requires a bit more time and training, usually requiring a full-time administrator. This means higher costs to maintain a domain environment.

Chapter 58

Sharing Resources

Windows will allow users to share almost everything—printers, CD-ROMs, files, folders, Zip drives, and even an Internet connection! The best part is the simplicity that Windows provides.

Share a Hard Drive or Folder

If you are in a networked environment, Microsoft has made sharing a hard drive or folder very simple to set up:

1. Right-click any hard drive or folder.

2. Select Sharing.

3. Click the Shared As radio button and give the share a name.

4. Click OK.

The next step is to see if that share is actually available to the network. On the PC hosting the share, open Network Neighborhood or My Network Places. Look for an icon with the name of the PC that is hosting the share. Double-click the icon and look for a folder with the share name you assigned. It is possible that you might have to look for the host PC in a workgroup or domain folder. It's just a matter of burrowing down deeply enough to find the host PC and the shared folder. Both a hard drive share and a folder share will appear the same; the hard drive will simply have more subfolders!

If you don't find the shared folder, double-check the drive or folder by right-clicking and choosing Sharing again. Make sure you've selected Shared As and given it an easy-to-find name. Also, after you've created a share, a small hand with a blue sleeve will appear under the drive or

Figure 58-1. These drivers are shared.

folder icon (see Figure 58-1). If you don't see this, it is possible that you have not enabled File and Print Sharing for your PC. File and Print Sharing must be installed and enabled for sharing to occur.

Share a Printer

Sharing a printer is about as easy as sharing a folder or drive. From the Control Panel, open the Printers folder and right-click the printer that you wish to share. Select Sharing, click Shared As, and give the printer a name (see Figure 58-2). With a shared printer, it is best to give the share a name that describes the printer. Names such as Laser400 or LasFloor3 are easier to figure out than Printer1 and Printer2.

The next step is to set up another PC to use that printer. Go to another PC on the network, open the Printers folder, and choose Add a Printer. This time, instead of installing a local printer, you will choose to install a network printer. You might need to browse around for the name of the printer in the Browse window, going into the workgroup or domain where the printer resides and finding the name you have given it. When you find it, you might be prompted for the printer driver CD or disk. After installing the printer software, the shared printer will be available from within applications for printing.

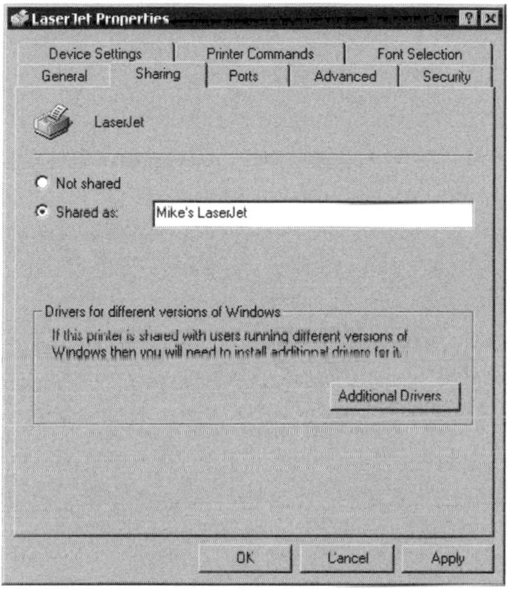

Figure 58-2. Share a printer

Chapter 59

TCP/IP

Transmission Control Protocol/Internet Protocol is a networking protocol suite (collection) that enables PCs, servers, and other devices to communicate. It is also the default protocol suite used for access to the Internet.

Binary Basics

TCP/IP talks in binary: collections of 1's and 0's. Workstations and servers identify themselves to each other via a 32-bit number. This number is called an IP address and is represented by a name to users and the world.

For example, a server might have an IP address of 192.168.1.20. This number isn't as easy to remember as, say, BIGBLUE1. But PCs and servers don't use either of these designations. BIGBLUE1 would actually communicate over the network and Internet using the following identifier:

11000000 10101000 00000001 00010010

This is a binary equivalent of 192.168.1.20. How is this achieved?

An 8-bit binary number can have 2^8 (256) permutations. If you break up that IP address number into four parts of 8 bits (called an octet) each, you get the following:

11000000   10101000   00000001   00010010

The value of an 8-bit binary number will fall between 0 and 255:

00000000 = 0

11111111 = 255

Therefore, a 32-bit binary address can range from 0.0.0.0 to 255.255.255.255. There are limitations on usable IP addresses, which disallows all 0's and all 1's in an octet, so IP addresses like 5.23.255.0 and 123.12.53.255 are illegal for general addressing. These are used for network (or subnet) numbers and broadcast addresses.

IP Components

TCP/IP provides the ability to network multiple devices, across multiple networks, in multiple locations. By giving devices a unique, addressable number, that device can be reached from anywhere in the world.

There are some key terms you need to be aware of when dealing with IP addresses:

- **Subnet mask**   A subnet mask allows an IP address to be examined to determine if it is a member of a local network (on the same network) or a remote network. PCs, servers, and other networked devices that are on the same network have a similar IP address when "filtered" through a subnet mask.

- **Default gateway**   To gain access to a remote network, a PC or other networked device uses a default gateway to communicate with the outside. Using the subnet mask, the default gateway determines whether to direct communication outside or keep it inside the network.

- **Dynamic Host Configuration Protocol (DHCP)**   IP addresses are running out. There are a finite number of public unique addresses in the 32-bit model, and when they're gone, they're gone. Manually assigning IP addresses on each networked device can be time-consuming. DHCP was created to help with these problems. Inside a local network, DHCP can be used to assign "private" IP addresses—these private addresses are only useful inside a local network. The default gateway will use a static, unchanging IP address, which is a valid, public, unique IP address that the rest of the world will recognize. The IANA has set aside some specific ranges of IP addresses for private use. These can be used by a network, but are not routable. The following are the ranges that are created for private use:

10.0.0.0 – 10.255.255.255
172.16.0.0 – 172.31.255.255
192.168.0.0 – 192.168.255.255

- **Domain Name Service (DNS)**   When a user wants to access a resource or web page, it is cumbersome to type in a 32-bit number every time. DNS allows the IP address to be resolved to a name. For example, BIGBLUE1 will be resolved to 11000000 10101000 00000001 00010010 for the behind-the-scenes network communications.

59

Chapter 60

Internet Connection Sharing

With Windows 98 Second Edition, Microsoft added a new feature called Internet Connection Sharing (ICS), shown in Figure 60-1. With ICS, multiple PCs running Windows 98 SE or later can share a single Internet connection.

Requirements for ICS to work include the following:

- Windows 98 SE or higher PC with one modem and one NIC (or two NICs) functioning as HOST

- One or more PCs running Windows 98 SE or higher, each with a NIC, functioning as CLIENT(s)

- A hub or switch to connect PCs together

- The PC acting as HOST must have Internet connectivity (dial-up, DSL, or other method)

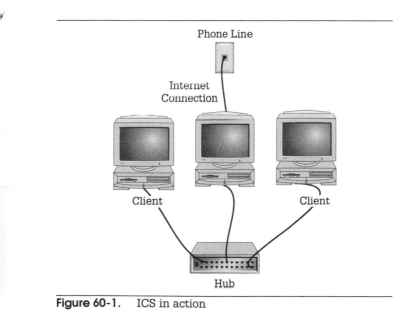

Figure 60-1. ICS in action

NOTE   *Obviously, one of these PCs must also be connected to the Internet!*

With Windows 98 SE, you have to install ICS from the Add/Remove Programs applet. ICS is found in the Internet Tools option under the Windows Setup tab.

ICS will assign a dynamic IP address to the clients using a private address pool that the HOST PC will manage. The client PCs will request access to the Internet, and the HOST machine will handle all Internet communications.

INTERNATIONAL CONTACT INFORMATION

AUSTRALIA
McGraw-Hill Book Company Australia Pty. Ltd.
TEL +61-2-9900-1800
FAX +61-2-9878-8881
http://www.mcgraw-hill.com.au
books-it_sydney@mcgraw-hill.com

CANADA
McGraw-Hill Ryerson Ltd.
TEL +905-430-5000
FAX +905-430-5020
http://www.mcgraw-hill.ca

GREECE, MIDDLE EAST, & AFRICA
(Excluding South Africa)
McGraw-Hill Hellas
TEL +30-210-6560-990
TEL +30-210-6560-993
TEL +30-210-6560-994
FAX +30-210-6545-525

MEXICO (Also serving Latin America)
McGraw-Hill Interamericana Editores S.A. de C.V.
TEL +525-117-1583
FAX +525-117-1589
http://www.mcgraw-hill.com.mx
fernando_castellanos@mcgraw-hill.com

SINGAPORE (Serving Asia)
McGraw-Hill Book Company
TEL +65-6863-1580
FAX +65-6862-3354
http://www.mcgraw-hill.com.sg
mghasia@mcgraw-hill.com

SOUTH AFRICA
McGraw-Hill South Africa
TEL +27-11-622-7512
FAX +27-11-622-9045
robyn_swanepoel@mcgraw-hill.com

SPAIN
McGraw-Hill/Interamericana de España, S.A.U.
TEL +34-91-180-3000
FAX +34-91-372-8513
http://www.mcgraw-hill.es
professional@mcgraw-hill.es

UNITED KINGDOM, NORTHERN,
EASTERN, & CENTRAL EUROPE
McGraw-Hill Education Europe
TEL +44-1-628-502500
FAX +44-1-628-770224
http://www.mcgraw-hill.co.uk
computing_europe@mcgraw-hill.com

ALL OTHER INQUIRIES Contact:
McGraw-Hill/Osborne
TEL +1-510-596-6600
FAX +1-510-596-7600
http://www.osborne.com
omg_international@mcgraw-hill.com